WHAT KANSAS MEANS TO ME

WHAT KANSAS MEANS TO ME

Twentieth-Century Writers on the Sunflower State

Edited and with an introduction by
Thomas Fox Averill

University Press of Kansas

© 1991 by the University Press of Kansas
See Acknowledgments for additional copyrights.

Published by the University Press of Kansas (Lawrence, Kansas 66049), which
was organized by the Kansas Board of Regents and is operated and funded by
Emporia State University, Fort Hays State University, Kansas State University,
Pittsburg State University, the University of Kansas, and Wichita State
University

Library of Congress Cataloging-in-Publication Data

What Kansas means to me: twentieth-century writers on the Sunflower
State / edited, with an introduction by Thomas Fox Averill.
     p.   cm.
Includes index.
ISBN 0-7006-0431-6 (cloth)   ISBN 0-7006-0710-2
1. Kansas.   2. Kansas—Poetry.   I. Averill, Thomas Fox, 1949–
F681.5.W47   1990   90-41688
978.1—dc20

British Library Cataloguing in Publication Data is available.

Printed in the United States of America

10 9 8 7 6 5 4 3 2

The paper used in this publication meets the minimum requirements of the
American National Standard for Permanence of Paper for Printed Library
Materials Z39.48-1984.

This book is dedicated to my teachers:

Wayne Wingo, who loved history, and taught me that Kansas was part of history, too;

Edgar Wolfe, who loved literature, and taught me that writers must always be aware of what has come before them;

Roy Gridley, who loved the level lands, and taught me that a region has many landscapes and many cultures;

Jennie Chinn, who learned Kansas, and taught me to observe familiar habits, and to call them folklore;

and to the many others who have helped me discover what Kansas means to me.

CONTENTS

ILLUSTRATIONS

PREFACE

This book began when Fred Woodward of the University Press of Kansas suggested the state needed a collection of well-written, affectionate, twentieth-century essays on the meaning and appeal of Kansas. Many nations, regions, and political entities have distinct cultural identities, and Kansans have been acutely conscious of an identity—both positive and negative—since territorial days. This book attempts to present some of the best positive thinking about who we are and why.

The essays and poems included here were selected from hundreds of writings about Kansas. Each treats the state as a whole, and each represents one part of a broad range of ideas about, interpretations and explanations of, and hopes for the Sunflower State. I paid particular attention to historical and literary writings for their focus on the concrete experiences traditional to Kansas: landscape, weather, historical event, cultural reality. I hope each essay will be inclusive enough to reach every Kansan, and I have suggested in my introduction and headnotes my sense of how each fits into the whole.

I would particularly like to thank Washburn University for its generous support of this project. University research grant funds made the preparation of this book possible; further, the Washburn University administration, as well as my colleagues there, have supported my writing, creative and scholarly, with their enthusiastic interest. Robert Stein, chair of the English Department, has welcomed Kansas Literature, Folklore, and Film into the department curriculum.

Besides my frequent consultations with Fred Woodward of the press, I appreciate my visits with C. Robert Haywood, and the hours of reading by, and talks with, my wife, Jeffrey Ann Goudie. Kelley Norman was responsible for most of the details of manuscript preparation; I admire her hard work, her quick intellect, and her efficiency. The staffs of Washburn University's Mabee Library and the Kansas State Historical Society Research Center were always available and timely in answering my many questions.

Finally, though, it is the writers themselves, many still living and working today, who made this book possible. Their generosity in giving permission (many with no remuneration) to reprint their work deserves the appreciation of any of you who find the book an addition to the Kansas experience, and your experience of Kansas.

Topeka, Kansas, 1990

INTRODUCTION: AFFLICTED BY AFFECTION

Thomas Fox Averill

Each working morning I rise at six A.M. and, with a cup of strong coffee, enter the private world of my upstairs study. I write. Most often, I write about Kansas, the setting of almost all my literary work, the subject of almost all my academic work. As I think, I often glance out the east-facing windows to check on the sunrise. Most mornings, the sky begins with the faintest shades of pink, moves to oranges and crimsons, then into the pale yellow of the morning sun.

Also to the east, the top of the State Capitol, its beacon light shining, glows radiant on the horizon. Washed in floodlights, its presence diminishes only as the sun rises to full strength and turns it into a gray silhouette. Finally, it becomes what it is: a green, copper-topped dome backed by pale blue Kansas sky.

Instead of a shade, a huge map of Kansas, discarded by the Topeka schools, hangs in my window to block the glare of the morning sun. Most mornings, it glows. I don't know when the map was published: it shows the Kansas Turnpike, but not Interstate 70; it shows Kanopolis, Cedar Bluff, and Kirwin Dams and Reservoirs, but not Tuttle Creek, Milford, and Perry. It shows land elevations, average rainfall, population density, and land use and mineral re-

Skyline, Topeka, Mary Huntoon

sources. It shows Kansas towns, some since given up the ghost (Dermot), railroad routes (C.B.&Q.), expedition routes (Pike's), trails (Chisholm), historic sites (Carry A. Nation's Home), commercial sites (World's Largest Natural Gas Field), Indian reservations (Kickapoo), air force bases (Sherman), and occupations (strip mining). Though the map is outdated, it is Kansas nevertheless. No matter its condition, it always reminds me of where I am.

Books about Kansas reassure me from my shelves. Photographs of Kansas remind me of the past and present here. Art by Kansas artists shows me some of the many responses to the place. On the floor is a hooked rug, rescued by a friend from a crumbling house near Clinton. The hole in its center will always be a hole; I don't intend to update

its condition any more than I plan to buy a new map. I like
Kansas, in all its different stages and manifestations, to surround me. This feeling about Kansas, this affection, this
sense that Kansas represents a state of mind is an affliction
I share with many Kansans. As historian C. Robert Haywood points out in "Kansas as a State of Mind" (in *The
Washburn Reader* [Topeka: Woodley Press, 1984], pp. 17–24):

> Others in the nation have made similar claims to terri-
> torial personification: Brooklynites before World War II,
> Texans now and forever, and the natives of the old Solid
> South. Kansas shares a little in common with these
> other peculiar states of mind: a twang perhaps, but no
> real discernible dialect; no uncomparable bigness and
> grandeur; and no Lost Causes. Still there is a certainty
> of identification.

Like many Kansans afflicted with this affectionate identification, I'm unsure of exactly when Kansas took hold of
me. I was raised in Kansas, in Topeka, during historically
conscious times. I came here from San Francisco, California, in 1953, and went to kindergarten in 1954, the year of
the Territorial Centennial. In 1961, during the Centennial
of Statehood, I was in sixth grade. We studied Kansas during those years. Our teachers read to us from the books of
Laura Ingalls Wilder, especially from *Little House on the
Prairie. The Wizard of Oz* was shown on television for the
first time in 1956, and the book, its copyright expired, was
republished in all sorts of newly abridged and illustrated
editions. Some weekends, using maps printed in the Sunday newspaper, my family, still new to Kansas, took trips to
historic sites like the Beecher Bible and Rifle Church and

drove scenic routes like the Mill Creek–Skyline Drive through the Flint Hills.

Still, it wasn't until I tried to write a historical novel set in Kansas that I first began studying Kansas novels and history: My own novel was a miserable failure, but the literature, folklore, and history of Kansas infected me with its state of mind. Some years later, when I attended the University of Iowa in 1975–76, I realized I would never live outside of Kansas again. So here I am, and here I plan to stay.

Such a proclamation may sound overdone, but other Kansans have made it, in the same way and perhaps for the same reasons. William Allen White remained always in Emporia because he believed in, and spent his life celebrating, the small town. Karl A. Menninger, with his father, C. F., and brother Will, started the Menninger Clinic in 1925 in Topeka because he believed it was a place of openness where his ideas about the humane treatment of the mentally ill would find sympathetic minds and hearts. Arthur Hertzler, after building and then operating one of Kansas' finest hospitals in Halstead for thirty years, wrote: "I . . . [showed] that in a small community a small hospital can be developed without the rigid commercial methods generally practiced. But to do this one must have Kansans and the Kansas spirit. . . . Your Kansan may fear God but he fears neither man nor the devil; neither grasshopper nor drought; bond salesman nor politicians, burglars nor bandits. Such . . . [Kansans] have made it possible for me to follow my plan even to this hour. This hospital is theirs because they built it" (Arthur Hertzler, *The Horse and the Buggy Doctor* [Lincoln: University of Nebraska Press, 1970], from Chapter 10). Historian Kenneth S. Davis, an expatriate Kansan, quotes a friend: "I've never met a Kansan anywhere whose heart wasn't buried in Kansas." Other, less published and less prestigious Kansans, myself included, make these same proclamations every day.

But why? If I cannot pinpoint just *when* Kansas took hold on me, I can also not pinpoint exactly *why*. This book represents an attempt. The first essay, "Kansas" by Carl Becker, was written in 1910 and opens with an incident that every Kansas historian can recite. Becker, on a train destined for Kansas, is seated near two young college women who, though bubbly in their talk all across Missouri, suddenly become silent as they cross into Kansas. With great feeling, one of them finally sighs and says, "Dear old Kansas!" Becker later wrote pages trying to understand that feeling. But it is a feeling that Kansans had almost from the beginning: a sense of place, a loyalty, a love, even, that at times seems almost incomprehensible, but which all who write about the state must try to understand, even today.

What Kansas Means to Me, then, is a collection of affectionate and acute essays and poems representative of the many, many attempts to understand Kansas and Kansans. Though varied in tone and form, though they come from different time periods, and from Kansans and non-Kansans, the seventeen pieces collected have one thing in common: the underlying assumption that there is something powerful, something significant, something noteworthy about Kansas.

This something may be part of the past: a combination of historical events and the mixture of people who struggled against great odds to settle and maintain decent, democratic lives and who succeeded.

This something may be part of the present: the shape and beauty of the land and sky, the Kansan's intimacy with the natural world of topography and with the weather, which Kansas poet John Moritz calls "vertical geography."

This something might also be defined in opposition to what surrounds Kansas: an industrialized, technological, urban world often overwhelming to those who must live in it and make sense of it.

Or, finally, this something might be the way in which all of these things weave together in the human body, mind, and spirit to create the Kansan for whom, as Becker writes: "Kansas is no mere geographical expression, but a 'state of mind,' a religion, and a philosophy in one."

One quality of this state of mind comes directly from the land. It is evidenced in the Native American response to the place, as a treaty speech of 1872 by Parra-Wa-Samen (Ten Bears) of the Yamparika Comanches demonstrates:

I was born on the prairie, where the wind blew free and there was nothing to break the light of the sun. I was born where there were no enclosures and where everything drew a free breath. I want to die there and not within walls. I knew every stream and every wood between the Rio Grande and the Arkansas. I have hunted and lived over that country. I lived like my fathers before me, and, like them, I lived happily.

William Allen White wrote similar words some fifty years later:

These things—the air, the water, the scenery and we who fill these scenes—hold many and many a man to Kansas when money would tempt him away. . . . Here are the still waters, here are the green pastures. Here, the fairest of the world's habitations.

These may seem like grandiose testimonials to the Kansas prairie, but both Parra-Wa-Samen and White are easily outdone by John Clum Bradshaw, who wrote: "God made the world, and rested. And then, to make creation doubly-sweet, he made the state of Kansas."

Others were enthusiastic about Kansas life in more general, but no less exaggerated, terms. The *Chicago Journal* wrote in 1889: "What Kansas will be 50 years hence is beyond the comprehension of people now living."

This enthusiasm for Kansas and its promise sometimes borders on the ludicrous. For example, in 1914 journalist Charles Harger of the *Abilene Reflector* proposed a Kansas Creed:

> We believe in Kansas, in the Glory of her Prairies, in the Richness of her Soil, in the Beauty of her Skies and in the Healthfulness of her Climate.
>
> We believe in the Kansas People, in their sturdy Faith and Abounding Enthusiasm, in their Patriotism and their Fidelity to the Good Things in Civilization, in their Respect for Law and their Love for Justice, in their Courage and Zeal, in their Independence and in their Devotion to Uplifting Influence in Education and Religion.
>
> We believe in Kansas Institutions, in the Kansas Language and in Kansas Ideals, in her Cleanliness of Society and in her demands that Honor, Sobriety and Respect be maintained in public and private life, in her Marvelous Productiveness and in her Wondrous Future.

And that's not all. Harger would have had Kansans continue that pledge until happiness would be in every home, making this "Commonwealth the Fairest in the Galaxy of States."

Certainly, the extremity of such praise and the demand for such loyalty might seem odd to those unschooled in Kansas history. Carl Becker and William Allen White, the first two writers in this book, give the best summary backgrounds on why the belief in the importance of Kansas was so strong both for Kansans and for nineteenth-century America as well. But W. G. Clugston, Milton S. Eisenhower, Allan Nevins, and Kenneth S. Davis also chronicle the landscape, the settlement, the history, and the culture of Kansas. Surprising as it might be, many of the historical analyses of Kansas start by establishing the connection between Kansas and America. "When anything is going to happen in this country, it happens first in Kansas," writes William Allen White. "The Kansas spirit is the American spirit, double distilled," writes Carl Becker. And W. G. Clugston begins his essay: "To say that a correct analysis of the cultural course of Kansas furnishes the formula for determining the course of civilization in the United States may be to take on the tincture of provincial egotism; but still, there may be more truth in such a statement than the ignorant provincial realizes."

Such claims for the importance of Kansas were not, of course, shared by everyone. Their seeming hubris can be countered almost immediately by their opposites. I think of novelist Earl Thompson's condemnation of the landscape in the opening of *Garden of Sand* ([New York: Signet, 1972], p. 9): "Love a place like Kansas and you can be content in a garden of raked sand." Or, as another antidote, the open-

ing of L. Frank Baum's *The Wizard of Oz*, in which gray
Kansas has squeezed all of the joy from Aunt Em and Uncle Henry. Or Junction City novelist Joseph Stanley Pennel's indictment of the Kansas people in his book about the post–Civil War settlement of Kansas: "But what sort of people squatted in Fork City anyway? They all sold each other wheat and bacon and corn and beef and farm machinery and squeaky shoes; they all talked in the same Goddamned flat nasal voice about the same Goddamned trivial things day-in-day-out year-after-year—eating, sleeping and growing more rustic and pompous and proverbial" (*The History of Rome Hanks and Kindred Matters* [New York: Scribner's, 1944], p. 3).

These are literary backlashes. And in fact, just as the historians and journalists are lauding Kansas (Becker and White are examples here), Kansas literary artists are at their most negative. Edgar Watson Howe's *The Story of a Country Town*, which shows the squalor of small-town Kansas life, precedes Becker's analysis by twenty years. Emanuel and Marcet Haldeman-Julius' *Dust* (New York: Brentano's, 1921) about a bitter, workaholic farmer whose life in Kansas adds up to nothing was published the year before White's essay. By the time the analysts are more negative (Eisenhower and Nevins are examples here), Kansas literary artists have become much more positive. So the political/ historical perception and the literary/cultural perception seem often at odds with each other, sometimes even within the same writer. C. Robert Haywood, quoted earlier, finishes his essay on Kansas with these words:

This love-hate ambivalence is the Kansas state of mind. It is fed by history, climate, land, and a mingling of races, religions, and philosophy. If we don't understand it, we have come to accept and appreciate it. If the clouds don't bring rain, nor the Federal government equity, nor the loud knock on our door opportunity, nor the stars all they promised, wait until next year. We'll still be here. We're staying.

In *What Kansas Means to Me*, I have tried for balance between the extremes of love and hate, praise and perfidy. Each piece is fundamentally appreciative of the state, but the case each builds is reasonable; there is logic and good sense amid the enthusiasm. Yes, most writers posit that Kansas is unique, interesting, politically important, beautiful in landscape and seasons. Most posit that Kansans are quintessential Americans, the "great common people," true residents of the heartland (the land of the heart). Such claims may sometimes sound overblown, even sentimental and corny. Yet the claim has so often been made for Kansas, and for Kansas in a way different from any other midwestern state, that it is worth exploring why.

From the beginning of settlement to the 1920s, most everything written seriously about Kansas is positive, or at least concedes Kansas' importance among the states of the nation. Ironically, after price increases during the First World War helped Kansas economically and during an economic boom in Kansas, writers began to express publicly their doubts about Kansas—its vitality, its importance, its future. It is as though a person sat down finally after years and years of work and questioned whether it had all been worth it. Prosperity gave people opportunities for things they hadn't had before: better education, more concern with cultural and social life, more time to travel and view a

Sod House, Logan County, Margaret Whittemore

larger world. The essays of White, Clugston, and Menninger all move from a positive beginning to a questioning of the present (1920s and 1930s). Each remains positive, for it is unwise to question whether the future can live up to the past if the past is in doubt.

The Crash of 1929 and the subsequent Dust Bowl resulted in a time Kansans knew as the Dirty Thirties. Drought, economic hardship, dust, lung disease, foreclosure: All were struggles Kansans were familiar with. Interestingly, the best book to come out of 1930s Kansas was by John Ise, *Sod and Stubble* (Lincoln: University of Nebraska Press, 1936), an account of pioneering in the Solomon Valley of Central Kansas, where Henry and Rosie Ise settled in 1873. John Ise, their son, a prominent economist at the University of Kansas, recalled the struggles of the pioneers. At one point, one of them says, "When we have rain and crops, we don't want to go, and when there ain't no crops we're too poor to go; so I reckon we'll just stay here till we starve to death" (p. 112). Ise is telling Kansans that their only choice in the 1930s is the choice of the 1870s and again of the 1890s: survival and, finally, triumph. Or, in Latin: *Ad Astra per Aspera*—"To the Stars through Difficulties."

The best poetry of the 1930s also harks back to the past. Poet-historian Kenneth Wiggins Porter shows the toughness of Kansas farmers through their humor:

> I'm over fifty—so I've seen it rain—
> Yeh, more than once—but there's my little grandson.
> He's five years old and if he don't see it rain
> Within a year or two, I'm might scared
> He'll have conniption fits when he does see it.

The past continues as the central theme in the essays by Eisenhower (1949) and Nevins (1954). Again, each challenges Kansas to a future that lives up to a proud past. Kenneth S. Davis, both in his "Portrait of a Changing Kansas" and in the longer history, *Kansas* (New York: Norton, 1976), puts the final cap on this particular positive chapter of Kansas analysis. Like the other essayists, he hopes the old horse can begin to run as fast as it did in its youth. Outsiders looking

in, including Neal R. Pierce and Jerry Hagstrom in *The*
Book of America: Inside the Fifty States Today (New York:
Norton, 1983), were less positive. Their chapter on Kansas
is titled "Kansas: The Eclipsed State." And by the 1970s
the *New Yorker* ran a cartoon showing an overpass sign on
an interstate highway. The sign reads, "You are now entering Kansas, or some state very much like it."

And by 1988, Kansan Robert Smith Bader, in his *Hayseeds, Moralizers, and Methodists: The Twentieth Century Image of Kansas* (Lawrence: University Press of Kansas, 1988),
writes:

> No state in the Union struggles more self-consciously
> with its image than Kansas. . . . Everyone agrees that,
> on balance, the image of Kansas is decidedly negative.
> Among young and old, natives and newcomers, Kan-
> sans and non-Kansans, the perception is universal that
> the state occupies an unenviable position in the na-
> tional psyche as a drab and backward society.

Bader demonstrates that images of Kansas, in the minds of
Kansans and non-Kansans alike, cluster around the following labels: Rube, Traditional, Drab, Irrelevant, and Puritanical.

But there are other important voices to hear, too. All of
the contemporary essays and poems, by Art Goodtimes,
Peg Wherry, William Least Heat-Moon, Robert Day, and
Denise Low, strike me as evidence that Kansas is not
eclipsed or irrelevant. In fact, what some of the earliest essayists wanted for Kansas is now happening: Kansas is creating an indigenous culture that matches the beauty, sub-
tlety, and quiet power of the state. In 1986, Kansas

novelist-biographer-historian Kenneth S. Davis spoke to a group of Kansas writers gathered for a conference in Topeka. Ten years before, in his essay "Portrait of a Changing Kansas," part of which appears in this collection, he had paraphrased William Allen White, saying that the cultural leaders of Kansas "had developed a profound inferiority complex, and perhaps with good reason since Kansas *had* become, in many ways, a backward state." But in 1986, after reading contemporary Kansas literature, he said:

> Your poems and stories, in many of which Kansas landscapes, Kansas weathers, Kansas people, distinctively Kansas attitudes—the sights and sound and *feel* of Kansas as a place to live and a living place—vividly impressed me.
>
> . . .
>
> The quality of Kansas higher education, the quality of Kansas journalism, the quality of Kansas politics, and certainly the Kansas economy and physical environment (Kansas as a place to live) . . . are all significantly improved, it seems to me and would, I think, have seemed so to William Allen White. I think he would have been delighted, as I have been, by the quality of literary work you people are doing and that he might have considered this evidence, as I do—might have considered the very fact that this writers' conference is being held as evidence—that the cultural renaissance which he wished for and I have long thought possible may now actually be underway.

Perhaps this new cultural appreciation of the region by its artists is a rebellion against the bicoastal cultural centers of

New York and Los Angeles, where many of the images
Robert Bader complains about are generated for us.

Perhaps it is a rebellion against our own stereotyping, as we wear our Wizard of Oz T-shirts and tease each other about our innocence by quoting the favorite line from *The Wizard of Oz*: "Toto, I have a feeling we're not in Kansas anymore." Novelist Robert Day both plays with and transcends such Kansas stereotypes in his recent *Washington Post Magazine* essay reprinted here.

Perhaps Kansas writers and artists are trying to bring the sense of place back to Kansas as a response to a political rush toward homogeneity. Politically, we *are* becoming like other states: With the institution of the lottery, parimutuel betting, and liquor-by-the-drink, we are trying to shuck the very images that Bader discusses. In doing so, we seem to be trying to please the rest of the country more than trying to be ourselves: the "great common people" Clugston celebrates; the "Puritan survival" White claims we represent; the "hybrid vigor" of North and South that Eisenhower sees in us. Given that, there may be more vision, vitality, and experimentation—and more to learn—from Kansas art than from Kansas politics.

In 1926, W. G. Clugston accused Kansas of two things: having a political system that required politicians to be either hypocrites or fanatics and not having made steps toward a true "art of living." In 1990, the "art of living," as understood by our poets, fiction writers, and artists, has perhaps made more progress than has the art of Kansas politics. Hence in the last essays in this collection, I have presented a selection of literary writers to show the fruition of the hopes of White, Clugston, Menninger, and Nevins. I

Old Cottonwood on State House Grounds, Topeka, Margaret Whittemore

hope to show a connecting thread between the earliest and most recent analyses of Kansas.

And, of course, my hope has been to understand *how* and *why* Kansas has its hold on so many people, including me. Now, even more than before I researched this volume, I'm not certain that I or anyone else can do that definitively. The history of this affection is long and complex. But I *can* say that every morning I look at the out-of-date map on my study wall. It reminds me of the historical past, mine and Kansas'. It inspires me to continue making sense

of the state and the state of mind I live in. And to understand the state, I must create it.

All of these writers create Kansas and, by so doing, make
Kansas a more comprehensible, a more interesting place.
Perhaps not the place John J. Ingalls claimed it was when
he wrote: "Kansas is indispensable to the joy, the inspiration, and the improvement of the world." But something
like that.

KANSAS

Carl L. Becker

*Carl Becker was born in Blackhawk County, Iowa, in 1873
and received both his B.A. and Ph.D. degrees in history from
the University of Wisconsin. He studied at Columbia University as well and taught at Dartmouth, the University of Kansas, and Cornell University, where he retired in 1941. He died
in Ithaca, New York, in 1945.*

*Although he lived in Kansas for only fourteen years, from
1902 to 1916, Carl Becker wrote, in 1910—at age 37 and only
three years after receiving his doctorate—what has become the
most quoted and often referred to analysis of the state. Titled
simply "Kansas," the essay brilliantly explains to the rest of
the country the "state of mind" of Kansas: a somewhat contra-
dictory combination of New England Puritanism, individualism, liberty, equality, conformity, materialism, and faith that is
the Kansas philosophy and religion. Becker calls Kansas history
"a succession of reverses and disasters" bearable only to those
"for whom defeat is worse than death, who cannot fail because
they cannot surrender." Of Kansas people, he writes: "With
Kansas history back of him, the true Kansan feels that nothing
is too much for him." And of Kansas politics: "Having conquered nature, [Kansans] cheerfully confront the task of transforming human nature" with a government they believe should
be "the individual writ large." Both scholarly and anecdotal,
"Kansas" provides a readable, still applicable perspective on
who we were and are, a perspective other writers on Kansas of-*

*ten acknowledge and echo as they explain, in their own ways,
what makes the Kansas state of mind.*

Some years ago, in a New England college town, when I informed one of my New England friends that I was preparing to go to Kansas, he replied rather blankly, "Kansas?! Oh." The amenities of casual intercourse demanded a reply, certainly, but from the point of view of my New England friend I suppose there was really nothing more to say; and, in fact, standing there under the peaceful New England elms, Kansas did seem tolerably remote. Some months later I rode out of Kansas City and entered for the first time what I had always pictured as the land of grasshoppers, of arid drought, and barren social experimentation. In the seat just ahead were two young women, girls rather, whom I afterwards saw at the university. As we left the dreary yards behind, and entered the half-open country along the Kansas River, one of the pair, breaking abruptly away from the ceaseless chatter that had hitherto engrossed them both, began looking out of the car window. Her attention seemed fixed, for perhaps a quarter of an hour, upon something in the scene outside—fields of corn, or it may have been the sunflowers that lined the track; but at last, turning to her companion with the contented sigh of a returning exile, she said *"Dear old Kansas!"* The expression somehow recalled my New England friend. I wondered vaguely, as I was sure he would have done, why any one should feel moved to say "Dear old Kansas!" I had supposed that Kansas, even more than Italy, was only a geographical expression. But not so. Not infrequently, since then, I have heard the same expression—not always from emotional young girls. To understand why people say "Dear old Kansas!" is to understand that Kansas is no mere geographical expression, but a "state of mind," a religion, and a philosophy in one.

The difference between the expression of my staid New England friend and that of the enthusiastic young Kansan, is perhaps symbolical, in certain respects, of the difference between those who remain at home and those who, in successive generations, venture into the unknown "West,"—New England or Kansas,—wherever it may be. In the seventeenth century there was doubtless no lack of Englishmen—prelates for example, in lawn sleeves, comfortably buttressed about by tithes and Thirty-nine Articles—who might have indicated their point of view quite fully by remarking, "New England?! Oh." Whether any New Englander of that day ever went so far as to say "Dear old New England," I do not know. But that the sentiment was there, furnishing fuel for the inner light, is past question. Now-a-days the superiority of New England is taken for granted, I believe, by the people who live there; but in the seventeenth century, when its inhabitants were mere frontiersmen, they were given, much as Kansans are said to be now, to boasting,—alas! even of the climate. In 1629, Mr. Higginson, a reverend gentleman, informed his friends back in England that "The temper of the aire of New England is one special thing that commends this place. Experience doth manifest that there is hardly a more healthful place to be found in the world that agreeth better with our English bodyes. Many that have been weake and sickly in old England, by coming hither have been thoroughly healed and growne healthfull strong. For here is a most extraordinarie cleere and dry aire that is of a most healing nature to all such as are of a cold, melancholy, flegmatick, rheumatick temper of body. . . . And therefore I think it a wise course for all cold complections to come to take physic in New England; for a sup of New England aire is better than a whole draft of Old England's ale." Now, we who live in Kansas know well that its climate is superior to any other in the world, and that it enables one, more readily than any other, to dispense with the use of ale.

There are those who will tell us, and have indeed often told us, with a formidable array of statistics, that Kansas is inhabited only in small part by New Englanders, and that it is therefore fanciful in the extreme to think of it as representing Puritanism transplanted. It is true, the people of Kansas came mainly from "the Middle West"—from Illinois, Indiana, Ohio, Iowa, Kentucky, and Missouri. But for our purpose the fact is of little importance, for it is the ideals of a people rather than the geography they have outgrown that determine their destiny; and in Kansas, as has been well said, "it is the ideas of the Pilgrims, not their descendants, that have had dominion in the young commonwealth." Ideas, sometimes, as well as the star of empire, move westward, and so it happens that Kansas is more Puritan than New England of to-day. It is akin to New England of early days. It is what New England, old England itself, once was—the frontier, an ever changing spot where dwell the courageous who defy fate and conquer circumstance.

For the frontier is more than a matter of location, and Puritanism is itself a kind of frontier. There is an intellectual "West" as well as a territorial "West." Both are heresies, the one as much subject to the scorn of the judicious as the other. Broad classifications of people are easily made and are usually inaccurate; but they are convenient for taking a large view, and it may be worth while to think, for the moment, of two kinds of people—those who like the sheltered life, and those who cannot endure it, those who think the world as they know it is well enough, and those who dream of something better, or at any rate, something different. From age to age society builds its shelters of various sorts—accumulated traditions, religious creeds, political institutions, and intellectual conceptions, cultivated and well kept farms, well built and orderly cities—providing a monotonous and comfortable life that tends always to harden into conventional forms resisting change. With all this the home-keeping and timid are well content. They sit in accustomed corners, disturbed by no fortuitous circumstance. But there are those others who are forever tugging at the leashes of ordered life, eager to venture into the unknown. Forsaking beaten paths, they plunge into the wilderness. They must be always on the frontier of human endeavor, submitting what is old and accepted to conditions that are new and untried. The frontier is thus the seed plot where new forms of life, whether of institutions or types of thought, are germinated, the condition of all progress being in a sense a return to the primitive.

Now generally speaking, the men who make the world's frontiers, whether in religion or politics, science or geographical exploration and territorial settlement, have certain essential and distinguishing qualities. They are primarily men of faith. Having faith in themselves, they are individualists. They are idealists because they have faith in the universe, being confident that somehow everything is right at the center of things; they give hostages to the future, are ever inventing God anew, and must be always transforming the world into their ideal of it. They have faith in humanity and in the perfectibility of man, [and] are likely, therefore, to be believers in equality, reformers, intolerant, aiming always to level others up to their own high vantage. These qualities are not only Puritan, they are American; and Kansas is not only Puritanism transplanted, but Americanism transplanted. In the individualism, the idealism, the belief in equality that prevail in Kansas, we shall therefore see nothing strangely new, but simply a new graft of familiar American traits. But as Kansas is a community with a peculiar and distinctive experience, there is something peculiar and distinctive about the individualism, the idealism, and the belief in equality of its people. If we can get at this something peculiar and distinctive, it will be possible to understand why the sight of sunflowers growing beside a railroad track may call forth the fervid expression, "Dear old Kansas."

I

Individualism is everywhere characteristic of the frontier, and in America, where the geographical frontier has hitherto played so predominant a part, a peculiarly marked type of individualism is one of the most obvious traits of the people. "To the frontier," Professor Turner has said, "the American intellect owes it striking characteristics. The coarseness and strength combined with acuteness and inquisitiveness; that practical, inventive turn of mind, quick to find expedients; that masterful grasp of material things, lacking in the artistic but powerful to effect great ends; that restless nervous energy; that dominant individualism, working for good and for evil, and withal that buoyancy

and exuberance that comes from freedom." On the frontier, where everything is done by the individual and nothing by organized society, initiative, resourcefulness, quick,
confident, and sure judgment are the essential qualities for
success. But as the problems of the frontier are rather restricted and definite, those who succeed there have necessarily much the same kind of initiative and resourcefulness,
and their judgment will be sure only in respect to the problems that are familiar to all. It thus happens that the type
of individualism produced on the frontier and predominant in America, has this peculiarity, that while the sense
of freedom is strong, there is nevertheless a certain uniformity in respect to ability, habit, and point of view. The
frontier develops strong individuals, but it develops individuals of a particular type, all being after much the same
pattern. The individualism of the frontier is one of achievement, not of eccentricity, an individualism of fact arising
from a sense of power to overcome obstacles, rather than
one of theory growing out of weakness in the face of oppression. It is not because he fears governmental activity,
but because he has so often had to dispense with it, that
the American is an individualist. Altogether averse from
hesitancy, doubt, speculative or introspective tendencies,
the frontiersman is a man of faith: of faith, not so much in
some external power, as in himself, in his luck, his destiny;
faith in the possibility of achieving whatever is necessary or
he desires. It is this marked self-reliance that gives to Americans their tremendous power of initiative; but the absence
of deep-seated differences gives to them an equally tremendous power of concerted social action.

The confident individualism of those who achieve
through endurance is a striking trait of the people of Kan-

sas. There, indeed, the trait has in it an element of exaggeration, arising from the fact that whatever has been achieved in Kansas has been achieved under great difficulties. Kansans have been subjected, not only to the ordinary hardships of the frontier, but to a succession of reverses and disasters that could be survived only by those for whom defeat is worse than death, who cannot fail because they cannot surrender. To the border wars succeeded hot winds, droughts, grasshoppers; and to the disasters of nature succeeded in turn the scourge of man, in the form of "mortgage fiends" and a contracting currency. Until 1895 the whole history of the state was a series of disasters, and always something new, extreme, bizarre, until the name Kansas became a byword, a synonym for the impossible and the ridiculous, inviting laughter, furnishing occasion for jest and hilarity. "In God we trusted, in Kansas we busted," became a favorite motto of emigrants, worn out with the struggle, returning to more hospitable climes; and for many years it expressed well enough the popular opinion of that fated land.

Yet there were some who never gave up. They stuck it out. They endured all that even Kansas could inflict. They kept the faith, and they are to be pardoned perhaps if they therefore feel that henceforth there is laid up for them a crown of glory. Those who remained in Kansas from 1875 to 1895 must have originally possessed staying qualities of no ordinary sort, qualities which the experience of those years could only accentuate. And as success has at last rewarded their efforts, there has come, too, a certain pride, an exuberance, a feeling of superiority that accompany a victory long delayed and hardly won. The result has been to give a peculiar flavor to the Kansas spirit of individual-

ism. With Kansas history back of him, the true Kansan
feels that nothing is *too much* for him. How shall he be
afraid of any danger, or hesitate at any obstacle, having
succeeded where failure was not only human, but almost
honorable? Having conquered Kansas, he knows well that
there are no worse worlds to conquer. The Kansas spirit is
therefore one that finds something exhilarating in the challenge of an extreme difficulty. "No one," says St. Augustine, "loves what he endures, though he may love to endure." With Kansans, it is particularly a point of pride to
suffer easily the stings of fortune, and if they find no pleasure in the stings themselves, the ready endurance of them
gives a consciousness of merit that is its own reward. Yet it
is with no solemn martyr's air that the true Kansan endures the worst that can happen. His instinct is rather to
pass it off as a minor annoyance, furnishing occasion for a
pleasantry, for it is the mark of a Kansan to take a reverse
as a joke rather than too seriously. Indeed, the endurance
of extreme adversity has developed a keen appreciation for
that type of humor, everywhere prevalent in the west,
which consists in ignoring a difficulty, or transforming it
into a difficulty of precisely the opposite kind. There is a
tradition surviving from the grasshopper time that illustrates the point. It is said that in the midst of that overwhelming disaster, when the pests were six inches deep in
the streets, the editor of a certain local paper fined his comment on the situation down to a single line, which appeared among the trivial happenings of the week: "A grasshopper was seen on the court-house steps this morning."
This type of humor, appreciated anywhere west of the Alleghenies, is the type *par excellence* in Kansas. Perhaps it has
rained for six weeks in the spring. The wheat is seemingly

ruined; no corn has been planted. A farmer, who sees his profits for the year wiped out, looks at the murky sky, sniffs the damp air, and remarks seriously, "Well, it looks like rain. We may save that crop yet." "Yes," his neighbor replies with equal seriousness, "but it will have to come soon, or it won't do any good." When misfortunes beat down upon one in rapid succession, there comes a time when it is useless to strive against them, and in the end they engender a certain detached curiosity in the victim, who finds a mournful pleasure in observing with philosophical resignation the ultimate caprices of fate. Thus Kansans, "coiners of novel phrases to express their defiance of destiny," have employed humor itself as a refuge against misfortune. They have learned not only to endure adversity, but in a very literal sense, to laugh at it as well.

I have already said that the type of individualism that is characteristic of America is one of achievement, not of eccentricity. The statement will bear repeating in this connection, for it is truer of Kansas than of most communities, notwithstanding there is a notion abroad that the state is peopled by freaks and eccentrics. It was once popularly supposed in Europe, and perhaps is so yet, that Americans are all eccentric. Now, Kansans are eccentric in the same sense that Americans are: they differ somewhat from other Americans, just as Americans are distinguishable from Europeans. But a fundamental characteristic of Kansas individualism is the tendency to conform; it is an individualism of conformity, not of revolt. Having learned to endure to the end, they have learned to conform, for endurance is itself a kind of conformity. It has not infrequently been the subject of wondering comment by foreigners that in America, where every one is supposed to do as he pleases, there should nevertheless be so little danger from violence and insurrection. Certainly one reason is that while the conditions of frontier life release the individual from many of the formal restraints of ordered society, they exact a most rigid adherence to lines of conduct inevitably fixed by the stern necessities of life in a primitive community. On the frontier men soon learn to conform to what is regarded as essential, for the penalty of resistance or neglect is extinction: there the law of survival works surely and swiftly. However eccentric frontiersmen may appear to the tenderfoot, among themselves there is little variation from type in any essential matter. In the new community, individualism means the ability of the individual to succeed, not by submitting to some external formal authority, still less by following the bent of an unschooled will, but by recognizing and voluntarily adapting himself to necessary conditions. Kansas, it is true, has produced its eccentrics, but there is a saying here that freaks are raised for export only. In one sense the saying is true enough, for what strikes one particularly is that, on the whole, native Kansans are all so much alike. It is a community of great solidarity, and to the native it is "the Easterner" who appears eccentric.

The conquest of the wilderness in Kansas has thus developed qualities of patience, of calm, stoical, good-humored endurance in the face of natural difficulties, of conformity to what is regarded as necessary. Yet the patience, the calmness, the disposition to conform, is strictly confined to what is regarded as in the natural course. If the Kansan appears stolid, it is only on the surface that he is so. The peculiar conditions of origin and history have infused into the character of the people a certain romantic and sentimental element. Beneath the placid surface there is something fermenting which is best left alone—a latent energy which trivial events or a resounding phrase may unexpectedly release. In a recent commencement address, Mr. Henry King said that conditions in early Kansas were *"hair-triggered."* Well, Kansans are themselves hair-triggered, slight pressure, if it be of the right sort, sets them off. "Every one is on the *qui vive*, alert, vigilant, like a sentinel at an outpost." This trait finds expression in the romantic devotion of the people to the state, in a certain alert sensitiveness to criticism from outside, above all in the contagious enthusiasm with which they will without warning espouse a cause, especially when symbolized by a striking phrase, and carry it to an issue. Insurgency is native in Kansas, and the political history of the state, like its climate, is replete with surprises that have made it "alternately the reproach and the marvel of mankind." But this apparent instability is only the natural complement of the extreme and confident individualism of the people: having succeeded in overcoming so many obstacles that were unavoidable, they do not doubt their ability to destroy quickly those that seem artificially constructed. It thus happens that while no people endure the reverses of nature with greater fortitude and good humor than the people of Kansas, misfortunes seemingly of man's making arouse in them a veritable passion of resistance; the mere suspicion of injustice, real or fancied exploitation by those who fare sumptuously, the pressure of laws not self-imposed, touch something explosive in their nature that transforms a calm and practical people into excited revolutionists. Grasshoppers elicited only a witticism, but the "mortgage fiends" produced the Populist regime, a kind of religious crusade against the infidel Money Power. The same spirit was recently exhibited in the "Boss Busters" movement, which in one summer spread over the state like a prairie fire and overthrew an established machine supposed to be in control of the railroads. The "Higher Law" is still a force in Kansas. The spirit which refused to obey "bogus laws" is still easily stirred. A people which has endured the worst of nature's tyrannies, and cheerfully submits to tyrannies self-imposed, is in no mood to suffer hardships that seem remediable.

II

Idealism must always prevail on the frontier, for the frontier, whether geographical or intellectual, offers little hope to those who see things as they are. To venture into the wilderness, one must see it, not as it is, but as it will be. The frontier, being the possession of those only who see its future, is the promised land which cannot be entered save by those who have faith. America, having been such a promised land, is therefore inhabited by men of faith: idealism is ingrained in the character of its people. But as the frontier in America has hitherto been geographical and material, American idealism has necessarily a material basis, and Americans have often been mistakenly called materialists. True, they seem mainly interested in material things. Too often they represent values in terms of money: a man is "worth" so much money; a university is a great university, having the largest endowment of any; a fine building is a building that cost a million dollars, better still, ten millions. Value is extensive rather than intensive or intrinsic. America is the best country because it is the biggest, the wealthiest, the most powerful; its people are the best because they are the freest, the most energetic, the *most* educated. But to see a materialistic temper in all this is to mistake the form for the spirit. The American cares for material things because they represent the substance of things hoped for. He cares less for money than for making money: a fortune is valued, not because it represents ease, but because it represents struggle, achievement, progress. The first skyscraper in any town is nothing in itself, but much as an evidence of growth; it is a white stone on the road to the ultimate goal.

Idealism of this sort is an essential ingredient of the Kansas spirit. In few communities is the word progress more frequently used, or its meaning less frequently detached from a material basis. It symbolizes the summum bonum, having become a kind of dogma. Mistakes are forgiven a man if he is progressive, but to be unprogressive is to be suspect; like Aristotle's non-political animal, the unprogressive is extra-human. This may explain why every Kansan wishes first of all to tell you that he comes from the town of X——, and then that it is the finest town in the state. He does not mean that it is strictly the finest town in the state, as will appear if you take the trouble to inquire a little about the country, its soil, its climate, its rainfall, and about the town itself. For it may chance that he is free to admit that it is hot there, that the soil is inclined to bake when there is no rain, that there is rarely any rain—all of which, however, is nothing to the point, because they are soon to have water by irrigation, which is, after all, much better than rainfall. And then he describes the town, which you have no difficulty in picturing vividly: a single street flanked by nondescript wooden shops; at one end a railroad station, at the other a post-office; side streets lined with frame houses, painted or not, as the case may be; a school house some-where, and a church with a steeple. It is such a town, to all appearances, as you may see by the hundred anywhere in the west—a dreary place which, you think, the world would willingly let die. But your man is enthusiastic; he can talk of nothing but the town of X——. The secret of his enthusiasm you at last discover in the inevitable "but it will be a great country some day," and it dawns upon you that, after all, the man does not live in the dreary town of X——, but in the great country of *some day*. Such are Kansans. Like St. Augustine, they have their City of God, the ideal-ized Kansas of some day: it is only necessary to have faith in order to possess it.

I cannot illustrate this aspect of Kansas idealism better than by quoting from Mrs. McCormick's little book of per-sonal experience and observation. Having related the long years of struggle of a typical farmer, she imagines the God-dess of Justice revealing to him a picture of "the land as it shall be" when justice prevails.

"John beheld a great plain four hundred miles long and two hundred miles wide—a great agricultural state covered with farmers tilling the soil and with here and there a city or village. On every farm stood a beautiful house handsomely painted outside and elegantly fur-nished inside, and equipped with all modern conven-iences helpful to housekeeping. Brussels carpets covered the floors, upholstered furniture and pianos ornamented the parlors, and the cheerful dining-room had elegant table linen, cut glass, and silverware. Reservoirs carried the water into the house in the country the same as in the cities. The farmers' wives and daughters, instead of working like slaves without proper utensils or house furnishings, now had everything necessary to lighten work and make home attractive. They had the summer kitchen, the wash-house, houses for drying clothes, arbors, etc. The door-yards consisted of nicely fenced green lawns, wherein not a pig rooted nor mule browsed on the shrubbery nor hen wallowed in the flower-beds. Shade trees, hammocks, and rustic chairs were scattered about, and everything bespoke comfort. Great barns sheltered the stock. The farms were fenced and subdivided into fields of waving grain and pastures green."

This is what John is supposed to have seen on a summer's day when, at the close of a life of toil, he had just been sold up for debt. What John really saw had perhaps a less feminine coloring; but the picture represents the ideal, if not an actual Kansas farmer, at least an actual Kansas woman.

This aspect of American idealism is, however, not peculiar to Kansas: it is more or less characteristic of all western communities. But there is an element in Kansas idealism that marks it off as a state apart. The origin of Kansas must ever be associated with the struggle against slavery. Of this fact, Kansans are well aware. Kansas is not a community of which it can be said, "happy is the people without annals." It is a state with a past. It has a history of which its people are proud, and which they insist, as a matter of course, upon having taught in the public schools. There are Old Families in Kansas who know their place and keep it—sacred bearers of the traditions of the Kansas Struggle. The Kansas Struggle is for Kansas what the American Revolution is for New England; and while there is as yet no "Soci-

John Brown, John Steuart Curry

ety of the Daughters of Kansas Struggle," there doubtless will be some day. For the Kansas Struggle is regarded as the crucial point in the achievement of human liberty, very much as Macaulay is said to have regarded the Reform Bill as the end for which all history was only a preparation. For all true Kansans, the border wars of the early years have a perennial interest: they mark the spot where Jones shot Smith, direct the attention of the traveler to the little village of Lecompton, or point with pride to some venerable tree bearing honorable scars dating from the Quantrill raid. Whether John Brown was an assassin or a martyr is a question which only a native can safely venture to answer with confidence. Recently, in a list of questions prepared for the examination of teachers in schools, there appeared the following: "*What was the Andover Band?*" It seems that very few teachers knew what the Andover Band was; some thought it was an iron band, and some a band of Indians. The newspapers took it up, and it was found that, aside from some of the old families, ignorance of the Andover Band was quite general. When it transpired that the Andover Band had to do with the Kansas Struggle, the humiliation of the people was profound.

The belief that Kansas was founded for a cause distinguishes it, in the eyes of its inhabitants, as pre-eminently the home of freedom. It lifts the history of the state out of the commonplace of ordinary westward migration, and gives to the temper of the people a certain elevated and martial quality. The people of Iowa or Nebraska are well enough, but their history never brought them in touch with cosmic processes. The Pilgrims themselves are felt to have been actuated by less noble and altruistic motives. The Pilgrims, says Thayer, "fled from oppression, and sought in the new world 'freedom to worship God.'" But the Kansas emigrants migrated "to meet, to resist, and to destroy oppression, in vindication of their principles. These were self-sacrificing emigrants, the others were self-seeking. Justice, though tardy in its work, will yet load with the highest honors, the memory of the Kansas pioneers who gave themselves and all they had to the sacred cause of human rights."

This may smack of prejudice, but it is no heresy in Kansas. The trained and disinterested physiocratic historian will tell us that such statements are unsupported by the documents. The documents show, he will say, that the Kansas emigrants, like other emigrants, came for cheap land and in the hope of bettering their condition; the real motive was economic, as all historic motives are; the Kansas emigrant may have thought he was going to Kansas to resist oppression, but in reality he went to take up a farm. At least, that many emigrants thought they came to resist oppression is indisputable. Their descendants still think so. And, after all, perhaps it is important to distinguish those who seek better farms and know they seek nothing else, from those who seek better farms and imagine they are fighting a holy war. When the people of Newtown wished to remove to Connecticut we are told that they advanced three reasons: first, "their want of accommodation for their cattle;" second, "the fruitfulness and commodiousness of Connecticut;" and finally, "*the strong bent of their spirits to remove thither.*" In explaining human history perhaps something should be conceded to "the strong bent of their spirits." Unquestionably cattle must be accommodated, but a belief, even if founded on error, is a fact that may sometimes change the current of history. At all events, the people of Kansas believe that their ancestors were engaged in a struggle for noble ends, and the belief, whether true or false, has left its impress upon their character. In Kansas the idealism of the geographical frontier has been strongly flavored with the notion that liberty is something more than a by-product of economic processes.

If Kansas idealism is colored by the humanitarian liberalism of the first half of the last century, it has nevertheless been but slightly influenced by the vague, emotional, Jean Paul romanticism of that time. Of all despondent and mystic elements, the Kansas spirit is singularly free. There are few Byrons in Kansas, and no Don Juans. There is plenty of light there, but little of the "light that never was on land or sea." Kansas idealism is not a force that expends itself in academic contemplation of the unattainable. It is an idealism that is immensely concrete and practical, requiring always some definite object upon which to expend itself, but once having such an object expending itself with a restless, nervous energy that is appalling: whatever the object, it is pursued with the enthusiasm, the profound conviction given only to those who have communed with the Absolute. It would seem that preoccupation with the concrete and the practical should develop a keen appreciation of relative values; but in new countries problems of material transformation are so insistent that immediate means acquire the value of ultimate ends. Kansas is a new state, and its inhabitants are so preoccupied with the present, so resolutely detached from the experience of the centuries, that they can compare themselves of to-day only with themselves of yesterday. The idea embodied in the phrase, "*Weltgeschichte ist das Weltgericht,*" has slight significance in a community in which twenty years of rapid material improvement has engendered an unquestioning faith in indefinite progress towards perfectibility. In such a community, past and future appear foreshortened, and the latest new mechanical device brings us an appreciable step nearer the millennium, which seems always to be just over the hill. By some odd mental alchemy it thus happens that the concrete and the practical have taken on the dignity of the absolute, and the pursuit of a convenience assumes the character of the crusade. Whether it be religion or paving, education or the disposal of garbage that occupies for the moment the focus of attention, the same stirring activity, the same zeal and emotional glow are enlisted: all alike are legitimate objects of conquest, to be measured in terms of their visual and transferable assets, and won by concerted and organized attack. I recall reading in a local Kansas newspaper some time ago a brief comment on the neighboring village of X—— (in which was located a small college mistakenly called a university), which ran somewhat as follows: "The University of X—— has established a music festival on the same plan as the one at the State University, and with most gratifying results. The first festival was altogether a success. X—— is a fine town, one of the best in the state. It has a fine university, and a fine class of people, who have made it a center of culture. X—— lacks only one thing; it has no sewers." Perhaps there are people who would find the juxtaposition of culture and sewers somewhat bizarre. But to us in Kansas it does not seem so. Culture and sewers are admittedly good things to possess. Well, then, let us pursue them actively and with absolute conviction. Thus may an idealized sewer become an object worthy to stir the moral depths of any right-minded community.

An insistent, practical idealism of this sort, always busily occupied with concrete problems, is likely to prefer ideas cast in formal mold, will be a little at a loss in the midst of flexible play of mind, and looks with suspicion upon the emancipated, the critical, and the speculative spirit. It is too sure of itself to be at home with ideas of uncertain pressure. Knowing that it is right, it wishes only to go ahead. Satisfied with certain conventional premises, it hastens on to the obvious conclusion. It thus happens that Americans, for the most part, are complaisantly [sic] satisfied with a purely formal interpretation of those resounding words that symbolize for them the ideas upon which their institutions are supposed to rest. In this respect Kansas is truly American. Nowhere is there more loyal devotion to such words as liberty, democracy, equality, education. But preoccupation with the concrete fixes the attention upon the word itself, and upon what is traditionally associated with it. Democracy, for example, is traditionally associated with elections, and many of them. Should you maintain that democracy is not necessarily bound up with any particular institution, that it is in the way of being smothered by the complicated blanket ballot, you will not be understood, or, rather, you will be understood only too well as advocating something aristocratic. Democracy is somehow bound up with a concrete thing, and the move for the shorter ballot is therefore undemocratic and un-American. Or, take the word socialism. Your avowed socialist is received politely, and allowed to depart silently and without regret. But if you tell us of the movement for the governmental control of corporate wealth, we grow enthusiastic. The word socialism has a bad odor in Kansas, but the thing itself, by some other name, smells sweet enough.

If one is interested in getting the essential features of socialism adopted in Kansas, or in America itself, the name to conjure with is indeed not socialism, but equality.

III

In a country like America, where there is such confident faith in the individual, one might naturally expect to find the completest toleration, and no disposition to use the government for the purpose of enforcing uniform conditions: logically, it would seem, so much emphasis on liberty should be incompatible with much emphasis on equality. Yet it is precisely in America, and nowhere in America more than in the west, that liberty and equality always go coupled and inseparable in popular speech; where the sense of liberty is especially strong, there also the devotion to equality is a cardinal doctrine. Throughout our history, the west has been a dominant factor in urging the extension of the powers of the national government, and western states have taken the lead in radical legislation of an equalizing character. This apparent inconsistency strikes one as especially pronounced in Kansas. The doctrine of equality is unquestioned there, and that governments exist for the purpose of securing it is the common belief. "A law against it" is the specific for every malady. The welfare of society is thought to be always superior to that of the individual, and yet no one doubts that perfect liberty is the birthright of every man.

Perhaps the truth is that real toleration is a sentiment foreign to the American temper. Toleration is for the skeptical, being the product of much thought or of great indifference, sometimes, to be sure, a mere *modus vivendi* forced upon a heterogeneous society. In America we imagine our-selves liberal-minded because we tolerate what we have ceased to regard as important. We tolerate religions but not irreligion, and diverse political opinion, but not unpolitical opinion, customs, but not the negation of custom. The Pu-ritans fought for toleration—for themselves. But having won it for themselves, straightway denied it to others. No small part of American history has been a repetition of the Puritan struggle; it has been a fight, not for toleration as a general principle, but for recognition of a civilization rest-ing upon particular principles: in exterior relations, a strug-gle for recognition of America by Europe; in interior rela-tions, a struggle for recognition of "the West" by "the East." The principle of toleration is written in our constitu-tions, but not in our minds, for the motive back of the fa-mous guarantees of individual liberty has been recognition of particular opinion rather than toleration of every opin-ion. And in the nature of the case it must be so. Those who create frontiers and establish new civilizations have too much faith to be tolerant, and are too thoroughgoing ideal-ists to be indifferent. On the frontier conditions are too hazardous for the speculative and the academic to flourish readily: only those who are right and are sure of it can suc-ceed. Certainly it is characteristic of Americans to know that they are right. Certainly they are conscious of having a mission in the world and of having been faithful to it. They have solved great problems hitherto unsolved, have realized utopias dreamed of but never realized by Europe. They are therefore in the van of civilization, quite sure of the direction, triumphantly leading the march towards the ultimate goal. That every one should do as he likes is part of the American creed only in a very limited sense. That it

is possible to know what is right, and that what is right
should be recognized and adhered to is the more vital belief.

That liberty and equality are compatible terms is, at all events, an unquestioned faith in Kansas. The belief in equality, however, is not so much the belief that all men are equal as the conviction that it is the business of society to establish conditions that will make them so. And this notion, so far from being inconsistent with the pronounced individualism that prevails there, is the natural result of it. In Kansas at least, no one holds to the right of the individual to do as he likes, irrespective of what it is that he likes. Faith in the individual is faith in the particular individual, the true Kansan, who has learned through adversity voluntarily to conform to what is necessary. Human nature, or, at all events, Kansas nature, is essentially good, and if the environment is right all men can measure up to that high level. That the right environment can be created is not doubted. It is not possible for men so aggressive and self-reliant, who have overcome so many obstacles, to doubt their ability to accomplish this also. Having conquered nature, they cheerfully confront the task of transforming human nature. It is precisely because Kansans are such thoroughgoing individualists, so resourceful, so profoundly confident in their own judgments, so emancipated from the past, so accustomed to devising expedients for every new difficulty, that they are unimpressed by the record of the world's failures. They have always thrived on the impossible, and the field of many failures offers a challenge not to be resisted.

To effect these beneficent ends, the people of Kansas turn naturally to the government because they have a very sim-

The Good Earth, John Steuart Curry

ple and practical idea of what the government is and what it is for. The government, in Kansas, is no abstract concept. It is nothing German, nothing metaphysical. In this frontier community no one has yet thought of the government as a power not ourselves that makes for evil. Kansans think of government, as they think of everything else, in terms of the concrete. And why, indeed, should they not? Within the memory of man there was no government in Kansas. They, Kansans, made the government themselves for their own purposes. The government is therefore simply certain men employed by themselves to do certain things; it is the sum of the energy, the good judgment, the resourcefulness of the individuals who originally created it, and who periodically renew it. The government is the individual writ large; in it every Kansan sees himself drawn to larger scale. The passion for controlling all things by law is thus not the turning of the hopeless and discouraged individual to some power other and higher than himself for protection; it is only the instinct to use effectively one of the many resources always at his command for achieving desired ends. Of a government hostile to the individual, they cannot conceive; such a government is a bogus government, and its laws are bogus laws; to resist and overthrow such a government, all the initiative and resourcefulness is enlisted that is devoted to supporting one regarded as legitimate. There is a higher law than the statute book; the law of the state is no law if it does not represent the will of the individual.

To identify the will of the individual with the will of society in this easy fashion, presupposes a certain solidarity in the community: an identity of race, custom, habits, needs; a consensus of opinion in respect to morals and politics.

Kansas is such a community. Its people are principally American born, descended from settlers who came mainly from the middle west. It is an agricultural state, and the conditions of life are, or have been until recently, much the same for all. "Within these pastoral boundaries," says ex-Senator Ingalls, in his best Kansas manner, "there are no millionaires nor any paupers, except such as have been deprived by age, disease, and calamity of the ability to labor. No great fortunes have been brought to the state and none have been accumulated by commerce, manufactures or speculation. No sumptuous mansions nor glittering equipages nor ostentatious display exasperates or allures." And the feeling of solidarity resulting from identity of race and uniformity of custom has been accentuated by the peculiar history of the state. Kansans love each other for the dangers they have passed; a unique experience has created a strong *esprit de corps*—a feeling that while Kansans are different from others, one Kansan is not only as good as any other, but very like the other. The philosophy of numbers, the doctrine of the majority, is therefore ingrained, and little sympathy is wasted on minorities. Rousseau's notion that minorities are only mistaken finds ready acceptance, and the will of the individual is easily identified with the will of society.

And in a sense the doctrine is true enough, for there is little difference of opinion on fundamental questions. In religion there are many creeds and many churches, but the difference between them is regarded as unimportant. There is, however, a quite absolute dogmatism of morality. Baptism is for those who enjoy it, but the moral life is for all. And what constitutes the moral life is well understood: to be honest and pay your debts; to be friendly and charitable, good-humored but not cynical, slow to take offense,

but regarding life as profoundly serious; to respect sentiments and harmless prejudices; to revere the conventional
great ideas and traditions; to live a sober life and a chaste
one,—to these they lay hold without questioning. Likewise
in politics. One may be democrat or republican, stalwart or
square-dealer, insurgent or stand-patter: it is no vital matter. But no one dreams of denying democracy, the will of
the people, the greatest good to the greatest number, equal
justice and equal opportunity to all. Whether in respect to
politics or economics, education or morals, the consensus
of opinion is very nearly perfect: it is an opinion that
unites in the deification of the average, that centers in the
dogmatism of the general level.

It goes without saying that the general level in Kansas is
thought to be exceptionally high. Kansans do not regard
themselves as mere westerners, like Iowans or Nebraskans.
Having passed through a superior heat, they are westerners
seven times refined. "It is the quality of piety in Kansas,"
says Mr. E. H. Abbott, "to thank God that you are not as
other men are, beer-drinkers, shiftless, habitual lynchers,
or even as these Missourians." The pride is natural enough,
perhaps, in men whose judgment has been vindicated at
last in the face of general skepticism. Having for many
years contributed to the gaiety of nations, Kansas has
ceased to be the pariah of the states. Kansans have endured
Job's comforters too long not to feel a little complaisant
[*sic*] when their solemn predictions come to naught. "While
envious rivals were jeering, . . . pointing with scorn's slow
unmoving finger at the droughts, grasshoppers, hot winds,
crop failures, and other calamities of Kansas, the world was
suddenly startled and dazzled by her collective display of

... products at the Centennial at Philadelphia, which received the highest awards." It is inevitable that those who think they have fashioned a cornerstone out of the stone rejected by the builders should regard themselves as superior workmen.

To test others by this high standard is an instinctive procedure. There is an alert attention to the quality of those who enter the state from outside. The crucial question is, are they "our kind of men?" Do they speak "the Kansas language?" Yet the Kansas language is less a form of speech, or the expression of particular ideas, than a certain personal quality. Some time since a distinguished visitor from the east came to the state to deliver a public address. He was most hospitably received, as all visitors are, whether distinguished or otherwise, and his address—permeated with the idealistic liberalism of a half century ago—was attentively listened to and highly praised. But to no purpose all these fine ideas. The great man was found wanting, for there was discovered, among his other impediments, a valet. It was a fatal mischance. The poor valet was more commented upon than the address, more observed than his master. The circumstance stamped the misguided man as clearly not our kind of man. Obviously, no man who carries a valet can speak the Kansas language. Needless to say, there are no valets in Kansas.

The feeling of superiority naturally attaching to a chosen people, equally inclines Kansans to dispense readily with the advice or experience of others. They feel that those who have worn the hair shirt cannot be instructed in asceticism by those who wear silk. In discussing the university and its problems with a member of the state legislature, I once hazarded some comparative statistics showing that a

number of other states made rather more liberal appropriations for their universities than the state of Kansas did for
hers. I thought the comparison might be enlightening, that
the man's pride of state might be touched. Not at all. "I
know all about that," he replied. "That argument is used
by every man who is interested in larger appropriations for
any of the state institutions. But it doesn't go with a Kansas legislature. In Kansas, we don't care much what other
states are doing. Kansas always leads, but never follows."
And, in fact, the disregard of precedent is almost an article
of faith; that a thing has been done before is an indication
that it is time to improve upon it. History may teach that
men cannot be legislated into the kingdom of heaven. Kansans are not ignorant of the fact, but it is no concern of
theirs. The experience of history is not for men with a mission and faith to perform it. Let the uncertain and the
timid profit by history; those who have at all times the
courage of their emotions will make history, not repeat it.
Kansans set their own standards, and the state becomes, as
it were, an experiment station in the field of social science.

The passion for equality in Kansas is thus the complement of the individualism and the idealism of its people. It
has at the basis of it an altruistic motive, aiming not so
much to level all men down as to level all men up. The
Kansan's sense of individual worth enables him to believe
that no one can be better than he is, while his confident
idealism encourages him to hope that none need be worse.

IV

The Kansas spirit is the American spirit double distilled. It
is a new grafted product of American individualism, Amer-

ican idealism, American intolerance. Kansas is America in microcosm: as America conceives itself in respect to Europe, so Kansas conceives itself in respect to America. Within its borders, Americanism, pure and undefiled, has a new lease on life. It is the mission of this self-selected people to see to it that it does not perish from off the earth. The light on the altar, however neglected elsewhere, must ever be replenished in Kansas. If this is provincialism, it is the provincialism of faith rather than of the province. The devotion of the state is devotion to an ideal, not to a territory, and men can say "Dear old Kansas!" because the name symbolizes for them what the motto of the state so well expresses, *ad astra per aspera*.

KANSAS:
A PURITAN SURVIVAL

William Allen White

*William Allen White (1868–1944) was one of the most promi-
nent Kansans of all time. Born in Emporia, raised in El Dorado,
he bought the* Emporia Gazette *in 1895 and declared that he
hoped to always sign himself William Allen White of Emporia.
He did. White's pen ranged well beyond the* Gazette, *into
poem, short story, novel, biography, and history. His politics
ranged from virulent anti-Populism into Progressive Republican-
ism. His travels took him all over the United States and the
world. Still, Kansas politics—with his 1896 diatribe against
Populism in "What's the Matter with Kansas"—won him his
first national audience, and his outlook always returned to
Kansas and Kansas concerns.*

*In "Kansas: A Puritan Survival," White explains, extolls,
and then questions a Kansas he is both proud of and worried
about. Demonstrating the state's Puritan penchant for abolitionism—of slavery, alcohol, tobacco, unsafe health practices,
even bad investments—White shows a Kansas settled into the
1920s: prosperous, democratic, law-abiding, economically egali-
tarian. White's final paragraphs, however, question whether
this society of "moral restrictions," that glorifies "God to
grease our busy dollars," might not be satisfying the mass of citizens at the expense of the few who could contribute the great
art, poetry, and philosophy Kansas might have to offer the na-*

tion and the world. White's fear is echoed politically in Nevin's "Kansas and the Stream of American Destiny" and culturally in Menninger's "Bleeding Kansans."

It is curious how State lines mark differences in Americans. There are no climatic differences between Kansas and Missouri, and small climatic differences between Kansas and Nebraska; yet the three States hold populations in which are marked differences—differences at least which Americans may distinguish. Doubtless to Chinamen all Americans look alike! But Americans know the differences between Americans North, East, South, and West, and dwellers in a section know minor differences between persons living in neighboring States in the same section of the United States. The larger sectional differences in Americans may be somewhat the result of climatic influences. But the distinguishing points between a Kansan and a Missourian, between a New Yorker and a citizen of Vermont, between a Georgian and a Virginian or a Louisianian, or between an Oregonian and a Southern Californian arise from the changes in men made by social and political institutions.

Kansans are marked by Puritanism. "Kansas," said our greatest statesman, John J. Ingalls, nearly forty years ago, "is the child of Plymouth Rock." In the beginning of the settlement of Kansas, the State was invaded by immigrants from New England or sons and daughters of New Englanders, who came to Kansas to make this a Free State. Congress left the question of slavery to the voters of the new State. A fair fight in an open field ensued; the abolitionists crowded out the proslavery people, outvoted them, and captured Kansas. The first Kansans, therefore, were crusaders, intellectual and social pioneers, converters of various sorts; which if you like to live comfortably upon your soft yesterdays, means that Kansas was full of cranks. Slavery being abolished your Kansans had to begin abolishing something else. Abolitionism was more than a conviction; it was a temperamental habit. It is a good or a bad habit according as you feel that you are your brother's keeper or that the devil should take the hindmost. Soldiers from the great war for the Union flooded into Kansas attracted by the free homesteads. But only Union soldiers could get free land, so Kansas was settled in the seventies and eighties almost exclusively by Northerners—partisans bitterly controversial and biologically marked by a blue stripe under the waistcoat; Yankees and children of Yankees. Something had to happen to Kansas with such a population. It happened. It was prohibition, adopted forty years ago. Curiously enough the Republican Party in Kansas always indorsed prohibition in its State platforms and through its candidates, while the Democratic Party, representing the feeble protest of the easy-going citizenship that had come in to Kansas in the fifties and sixties bringing slaves, opposed prohibition. But the Democratic minority was negligible and the prohibitionists took away the liquor of their less scrupulous neighbors as their slaves had been taken. For two decades the prohibition problem engaged Kansas. It was a hard fight, but it never wavered. The Puritan won. The Law and Order League in every town and county worked day and night, and to make the victory surer five years after prohibition came in, the State allowed women to vote in municipal matters, and women having the ballot in the towns where liquor was sold never stopped until prohibition succeeded. It required laws which permitted search and seizure, which prohibited doctors prescribing liquor, and druggists from keeping it in stock, laws which permitted the confiscation of liquor-running automobiles, and which made the second offense of the liquor seller a felony, sending him to the penitentiary for it—but in the end, prohibition won. Your Puritan is no slouch; he is thorough at all costs; thorough and fairly consistent.

For then came Populism. Populism had its genesis in the South probably; and it ran a mild course in the Dakotas and Colorado and Nebraska, States all more or less like Kansas in climate, in economic status, and in blood and breed. But because of the blood and breed, because of the Puritan inheritance of Kansas, the dour deadly desire to fight was deemed wrong for the sheer sake of obliterating wrong. Kansas took Populism much more seriously than her sister States. Kansas produced most of the leadership of Populism. And long after Populism was defeated and forgotten Kansas clung to it, adopted its creed, and forced a dilution of Populism upon an unwilling nation. The insurgence of insurgency, the progressiveness of the Bull Moose, was the restless spirit of Kansas trying to realize the dream of Populism. Murdock, Bristow, Stubbs, Allen and Capper in the uprising of the first two decades of the century gave to the national movement a certain blind crusader's enthusiasm. It was with a ghoulish grin that Victor Murdock met a fellow Kansan the morning when Roosevelt threw his hat into the ring in 1912.

"Well—he's finally in," said the Kansan.

"And it's a fine joke on him," says Victor.

"Why?" says the Kansan.

"Because he thinks it's '60 and it's only '48," chuckled

the Puritan, delighted that a great man was to aid a good
cause and go to defeat in it, even if the great man did not
dream what was ahead of him.

That was the Kansas of it. Murdock had no remote
thought of hesitating because he saw the inevitable defeat.
Defeat was his meat and drink. But he had his sneaking
doubts about the Puritan zeal of Roosevelt, who was practical Dutch, doughty, and gorgeously militant; but with a sly
sweet tooth for victory and its fruits. Your Puritan regards
any sweet tooth as a weakness bordering upon sin! So Kansas has delighted in causes rather than conquests.

After prohibition succeeded and Populism passed, the pioneer spirit of Kansas engaged itself in several social and
political experiments, most revolutionary then; but now
they have become sane and commonplace attitudes in the
ordinary way of life. The theory, for instance, that the
State has a right to interfere in the individual's habits on
behalf of the better health of the people of the State. Under the State Board of Health which had unusual police
powers Kansas abolished the common drinking cup and
the roller towel from public places, took over the distribution of various toxins against contagious diseases, in-
spected hotels and food stores, and closed them up when
they were unsanitary. The State also guaranteed bank deposits and restricted the sale of stocks and bonds to proj-
ects that had State approval; established a State hospital
where crippled children may be cured at State expense;
printed its own school textbooks and distributed the books
at cost; tightened its grip on public utilities operating in the
State; passed a law which virtually socializes all Kansas industry except agriculture, and passed the long line of legislation, once referred to as socialistic and now merely

sneered at as laws of Meddlesome Mattie, but accepted by most of the progressive States of the Union and loudly bewailed by those who believe in the laissez-faire theory of morals and economics.

Kansas delighted in being among the first to pass all of these and actually the first to enact many of them. Again it was the Puritan spirit cropping out. Prohibition had kept out of Kansas hundreds of thousands of Germans and Scandinavians and Bohemians who flooded Nebraska and the Dakotas in the eighties and nineties, and the New England strains of blood continued to dominate the life of the State. Nearly 77 per cent of our population is of American-born parents. The Puritan blood even now is the strongest current—almost the only current directing our thought in Kansas. We censor the movies and prohibit them on Sundays. We forbid race-track gambling—indeed gambling of all kinds is illegal; stop the sale of cigarettes—or try to. We permit Sunday baseball, but only because it is amateur sport and is not commercialized. We prohibited the thing called white slavery before the passage of the Mann Act, and commercialized prostitution has been stopped in Kansas, as entirely as commercialized horse-stealing or commercialized arson or commercialized larceny of any kind. All these inhibitions against the natural tendency of depraved man cut loose from the apron-strings we are pleased to call moral restrictions. We make the questions moral issues arising before and after the passage of our restrictive laws. We go to the churches and schools for our political majorities. The politician who tries to assemble a majority without the churches and schools, without the women, without what is known as the best influences in the community always finds himself leading a minority. He rails at

the long-haired men and short-haired women; he rages at
the Pecksniffian attitude of life. But it is deeply ingrained in
the Kansas character. It seems so infernally pious; so hypocritical to those who oppose these causes. Yet at base these
questions—abolition, prohibition, health, stability of sav-
ings, cigarettes, prostitution, gambling, and social and industrial justice—are not moral but economic in their value
to society. Slavery would not work in a modern world; neither does the saloon; cigarettes and common drinking cups
and prostitutes and roller towels and impure foods and
long working hours cut down the producing power of men,
cripple their economic efficiency; so puritanism which is always keen about the main chance makes a cause out of
abolishing them, sings hymns—as, for instance, "Onward,
Christian Soldiers," or "Where is my Wandering Boy Tonight," or "The Slave's Lament"—and quotes texts and
holds prayer meetings to gild the main chance with the
golden glow of piety. But after all it is the main chance the
Puritan is after. He is an idealist planning a great democratic civilization; but one wherein a dollar will travel further, work harder, and bring in more of the fruits of civilization than any other dollar in the world. The waste of
slavery, the social expense of the saloon, the venereal disease, the crooked stock seller, the purveyor of expensive
schoolbooks or impure food, or the dishonest banker—
each immediately becomes a check to the Puritan scheme
of things and automatically is invested with evil! Meddlesome Mattie is the machinist operator who is forever listening into the works to hear a knock or a bur-r-r; and hear-
ing it, jabs her monkey wrench into a lot of fun for some
one, not because it is fun, but because it costs too much to
maintain the bad adjustment.

So much for the institutions of Kansas—for her society and politics. Now for the life of Kansas, for which she has instituted her laws and social standards and upon which they rest. What manner of people are these Puritans who sing hymns and quote texts and glorify moral issues to cover the main chance, who glorify God to grease their busy dollars? As a pragmatic proposition does their civilization work? Is it worth while? Are people freer, happier, more prosperous, more comfortable and wise under this order of things than they are under the scheme of things which shrugs its Latin shoulders and says it does not care; says to waste is human, to enjoy divine? First let us look at the material side. As to wealth, for instance. Ten years ago the figures indicated that the county in the United States with the largest assessed valuation was Marion County, Kansas, a county in central Kansas, not materially different from any other county; Marion County happened to have a larger per capita of bank deposits than any other American county. Its average of per capita wealth and per capita bank deposits was not much higher than the Kansas average. Yet no man in Marion County was then rated as a millionaire, but the jails and poorhouses were practically empty. The great per capita of wealth was actually distributed among the people who earned it. They were sober, so they saved; they were healthy, so they worked. They were well schooled, so they worked to purpose and with direction and made money. They were clear-brained, well-bred, cold-blooded Yankees, who knew exactly what they wanted, how to get it and where to put it. That is your Kansan. Typically he lives either upon an eighty-acre farm or in a detached house within a fifty-foot lot, near a schoolhouse, with an automobile in the garage, whether farmer or town dweller; if a farmer he lives upon a rural free-delivery route along which the postman brings to him at least one daily paper, one weekly paper, and one monthly; if a town dweller he lives upon a paved street, a sewer line, a telephone wire, an electric light and power conduit and a gas main. In the county wherein these lines are written, an ordinary Kansas county, the number of telephones exceeds the number of families, the daily newspaper prints as many copies as there are heads of families and in the towns the number of electric light connections is more than the number of residences. Water and gas are common and the bank deposits for the town and county are $6,260,000 and the number of depositors 21,500 in a county with the total population of 26,496 people. Ninety per cent of the families are within five miles of a high school in this county, and 25 per cent of the children of high-school age attend the high school. The county contains two colleges and the attendance from the county in the colleges is 623! A farm agent who receives $2,200 a year advises the farmers about crops, helps them to overcome bugs and pests, and organizes them for marketing. The county is spending a quarter of a million upon its own hospital and no citizen of the county is in jail. Twenty-five miles of hard-surfaced roads are under construction and as much more ordered in. It costs less than $2,000 last year to try all the criminals that infest the courts, and a preacher is police judge of the county-seat town. He commits less than a dozen men a year to jail—and this in a town of 12,000 surrounded by a county of 26,496.

This is a Kansas average, and there is your ideal Puritan civilization: a prosperous people, burdened neither by an idle and luxurious class who are rich, nor taxed to support

Industrial Wichita #2, William Dickerson

a sodden and footless class verging upon pauperism. A sober people practically without a criminal class, an intelligent people in so far as intelligence covers a knowledge of getting an honest living, saving an occasional penny, and living in a rather high degree of common comfort; a moral people in so far as morals consist in obedience to the legally expressed will of the majority with no very great patience for the vagaries of protesting minorities. A just and righteous people in so far as justice concerns the equitable distribution of material things, and righteousness requires men to live at peace among men of good-will. A free people

in so far as freedom allows men and women to have and
hold all that they earn, and makes them earn all that they
get. But a people neighbor minded in the Golden Rule, a
people neighbor bound by ties of duty, by a sense of obligation, by a belief in the social compact, in the value of the
herd, in the destiny of the race. All these social totems are
concentrated in the idea of God in the Kansas heart. We
are a deeply religious people. Time was when they used to
say in Kansas that the Republican Party and the Methodist
church were the spiritual forces that controlled the State.
"Ad astra per aspera," to the stars by hard ways, is the
State motto, and kindly note the "hard ways." Ours is no
easy approach to grace, no royal road to happiness, no
backstairs to beneficence. There is no earthly trail parallel-
ing the primrose path in which one can avoid the wrath of
God and the lady next door. Life and liberty are indeed
highly esteemed in Kansas; but the pursuit of happiness
only upon conditions set forth in the Ten Command-
ments, the Golden Rule, and their interpretation by the
Kansas statutes.

Still we are not a joyless people. We laugh easily, and for
the most part kindly. But we often approve the things we
laugh at; we laugh one way and vote another. Our sense of
humor saves us, but not entirely whole; we have never
laughed ourselves out of our essential Puritanism. Laughter
as a solvent has been tried—the anti-prohibitionists tried
it, the opponents of Populism tried it, the defenders of
Cannon and Aldrich and conservatism tried it. But they
all failed as flatly as the Missourians and the gay Southerners failed who tried to laugh at the abolition rifles by dub-
bing them "Beecher's Bibles." Deep in our hearts is the ob-
sessed fanaticism of John Brown. Joy is an incident, not the

business of life. Justice as it works out under a Christian civilization is the chief end of man in Kansas.

But alas, this is begging the question. For who can say that the establishment of justice is the chief end of a state? Indeed who can say even what justice is? Is it just that every man should earn what he gets and get what he earns? Or is it just that those who see and feel and aspire to do great things—to make life beautiful for themselves and others—should be pared down to the norm in their relations with mankind? Is it justice to establish a state where the weak may thrive easily and the strong shall be fettered irrevocably in their most earnest endeavors? Should a state brag of the fact that it distributes its wealth equitably—almost evenly—when it has produced no great poet, no great painter, no great musician, no great writer or philosopher? Surely the dead level of economic and political democracy is futile if out of it something worthy—something eternally worthy—does not come. The tree shall be known by its fruit. What is the fruit of Kansas? Is happiness for the many worth striving for? What is the chief end of a civilization? What is the highest justice?

What we lack most keenly is a sense of beauty and the love of it. Nothing is more gorgeous in color and form than a Kansas sunset; yet it is hidden from us. The Kansas prairies are as mysterious and moody as the sea in their loveliness, yet we graze them and plow them and mark them with roads and do not see them. The wind in the cottonwoods lisps songs as full of meaning as those the tides sing, and we are deaf. The meadow lark, the red bird, the quail live with us and pipe to us all through the year, but our musicians have not returned the song. The wide skies of night present the age-old mystery of life, in splendor and baffling magnificence, yet only one Kansas poet, Eugene Ware, has

ever worn Arcturus as a bosom pin. The human spirit— whatever it is in God's creation—here under these winds and droughts and wintry blasts, here under these drear and gloomy circumstances of life, has battled with ruthless fate as bravely and as tragically as Laocoon; yet the story is untold, and life no richer for the nobility that has passed untitled in marble or in bronze or in prose. Surely the righteousness which exalts a nation does not also blind its eyes and cramp its hands and make it dumb that beauty may slip past unscathed. Surely all joy, all happiness, all permanent delight that restores the soul of man, does not come from the wine, women, and song, which Kansas frowns upon.

Yet why—why is the golden bowl broken, the pitcher at the fountain broken, and in our art the wheel at the cistern still? This question is not peculiarly a Kansas question. It is tremendously American.

KANSAS, THE ESSENCE OF TYPICAL AMERICA

W. G. Clugston

William George Clugston (1889–1966) was born and raised in Kentucky, graduating from the University of Kentucky in law and then becoming a journalist. He worked on the staffs of the Topeka State Journal, the Kansas City Star, and the Kansas City Journal. He was also editorial correspondent for the New York Times and wrote for H. L. Mencken's American Mercury, the Nation and other magazines. His books were Rascals in Democracy, about Kansas politics, a play, Animal Crackers, and several titles published in the Little Blue Book series by Emanuel Haldeman-Julius of Girard.

Like other Kansans in the 1920s, Clugston was concerned about the direction of the state and the nation. Like other Kansans, he believed that Kansas was a kind of barometer: know Kansas and thus know the nation as a whole. Unlike other Kansas analysts, Clugston viewed Kansans as a "proletariat," the common people, whose ancestors were primarily Southern "po' white trash" interested in creating a casteless society and insuring economic equality for themselves after generations of exclusion from a Southern aristocratic system based on "black vassalage." Though undocumented and exaggerated, Clugston's "po' white trash" theory leads him to the same conclusion as other Kansas analysts, that Kansans represent the great struggle for true democracy and equality, and, by the 1920s, Kansas seems successful.

Clugston has the usual complaints about Puritanism and "political claptrappery," which turn any politician into either a hypocrite or a fanatic (this may still be true in Kansas), but he is most interested in the future: Will Kansas and the United States move from newfound economic prosperity to the next frontier, that of cultural awakening and a concern with the "art of living?" In asking these questions, Clugston echoes William Allen White, though from a very different political perspective. And if Karl Menninger's 1939 essay, "Bleeding Kansans," can be read as a response to Clugston, his answer is, "No, Kansans have not yet found out the art of living."

If Oswald Spengler had been born and raised in Olmitz, Kan., and if he had been educated at the Kansas State Agricultural College at Manhattan, and if he were today occupying the chair of history at Kansas University—if all these things could be, what future would he see for the Sunflower State? What would he have to say about the morphology of Kansas culture—the development, or decline, of the social structures which came into being and took form during the agitations of John Brown, which crystallized into Populism and Prohibition under "Sockless" Jerry Simpson, Mary Ellen Lease and Carry Nation, and which, apparently, have begun to melt into new moulds with the decline of the political prestige of such outstanding Progressive[s] as Henry J. Allen, William Allen White, Victor Murdock and J. L. Bristow?

If our whole civilization is going to the dogs, as Spengler attempts to show in *The Decline of the West*, Kansas must be going there too. But to those of us who are one-age individuals, and who call Kansas "home," the general course of the marching armies of civilization is not so important as the position in the procession occupied by our particular coterie of troopers. Are we of Kansas leading the vanguard of our division? Are we in the rear struggling to keep up? Or are we making a feeble or a forceful effort to start a flank movement which may, in time, draw us away from disaster?

To say that a correct analysis of the cultural course of Kansas furnishes the formula for determining the course of civilization in the United States may be to take on the tincture of provincial egotism; but still, there may be more truth in such a statement than the ignorant provincial realizes. Assuming that the destiny of our Republic is to be shaped by her *great common people*, there is reason to give attention to the morphology of Kansas because no State in the Union has been more generally domiciled and dominated by the average, ordinary individual generally referred to as the common people. In matters of politics, economics, education and industry the ideas and ideals of the *common people* have prevailed in Kansas as in no other State. As far back as 1883 "Main Street" was such a manifest thing in Kansas that Ed Howe was able to write *The Story of a Country Town,* and to put into it every commonplace that Sinclair Lewis, Sherwood Anderson and their imitators have been able to put into their modern pictures of American life. I do not mean that in Kansas the percentage of commoners today is measurably greater than the percentage in Connecticut or Colorado, but their aims and inclinations are more nearly attained and their mental and spiritual attitudes are more nearly ascendant.

The Commonwealth of the Kaw has occupied so much general attention, and has been so prominently identified with Progressive and Puritanical crusades and uprisings that prides and prejudices well-nigh made enigmas of the inspirational activities of her leaders. How much is Puritanism responsible for the unique place the State occupies in current history? How much has the climate had to do with forming the character and the cravings of the people? To what extent have the constantly blowing winds of the Western plains been responsible for the political uprisings—winds that produce a constant irritant, making men restless and more ready to take a chance than they would be in a quiet, peaceful atmosphere? How much has the lack of social caste lowered the level of leadership?

All these questions must be taken into consideration in determining the factors that have made Kansas what she is today, and incline the State to what it will be tomorrow. But I am convinced the major factor in the development of the peculiarity of this political entity has been the character of the people who first settled the territory—the inclination and the aspirations of the pioneers who put the State on the map and produced a social order while they were plowing under the buffalo chips and shooting prowling Indians.

THE FIRST SETTLERS

The settlement of Kansas and the settlement of the Civil War controversy were concurrent. By far the most of those who came into this State in the early days of the slavery struggle were "poor whites" from the South. There were, it is true, members of the Massachusetts colony and other

New Englanders, as well as settlers from Illinois, Iowa and other Northern States; but the majority came from the Southland. In the States from which they had come these men and their families had been forced into the lowest stratum of society. Having no slaves and little or no land, they were looked upon as nobodies; they were commonly called "po' white trash" and were despised, even by the negro slaves. They were held down by a caste system built upon an aristocracy which was maintained by black vassalage. Naturally, they blamed slavery for the hard life forced upon them in their home States. When they came to Kansas and saw a chance to make a State where the evils of slavery would never exist they set about the task in the most fanatical manner, and were willing to go to any lengths to protect themselves and their posterity from the degrading existence they had fled. In the slavery struggle these Southern settlers were, by all odds, the most rabid of the Kansas Abolitionists, and, while they were not so prominent as leaders, they furnished the predominance of numbers to make their cause prevail.

Uniting forces with the New England Puritans, the "po' white trash" from the South fought the pro-slavers on all sides, and the two forces, having many ideas and ideals in common, proceeded to shape the State to their liking. Always they insisted upon equalities. They were everlastingly struggling to prevent the growth of a caste system—to make the *great common people* supreme. Whenever a group appeared to be getting too powerful a "boss buster" movement would be launched with a political upheaval following. Some one's head was always being chopped off, politically speaking, and the only certain way for a politician to get to the front was through a loud-mouthed championing of the cause of the *great common people*.

There is no greater proof of the continuing influence of this attitude than the Kansas idolatry of the late William Jennings Bryan. There has never been a national people's idol who has had such a hold on the people of Kansas as Bryan had. He carried the State in 1896, and, up to the time of his death, every time he came into a community his presence caused a near-riot of enthusiasm. He was loved as no public figure since Lincoln.

Political manifestations do not necessarily indicate the trend of the social order, but when a whole people becomes absorbed in politics to the exclusion of other interests this may be taken to indicate one of two things—a lack of capacity for more edifying activities or an irritating dissatisfaction with the existing state of affairs coupled with a belief that a political change will bring improvements.

Since the inception of the State, Kansas has expressed herself most noticeably through political articulations. In the arts and sciences she has seldom been either a leader or a laggard: but there have been few political uprisings in which her people have not played a conspicuous part. I shall not attempt to say which of the two causes cited above has been responsible, but it is a fact that before the Corn Belt crusade of 1926 there has been no widespread revolt in which Kansas has not essayed a leading role. Bryan and the Free Silver furor, the Bull Moose bolt and the Wilson wave, all swept Kansas and established main strongholds in the Sunflower State.

Only within the last decade has the political consciousness of the people appeared to be losing its prominence. True, the progressivism which put the Bull Moose move-

ment on the national stage survived here long after the re-
action had set in elsewhere, but the unmistakable end
came to this manifestation with the close of the administration of Governor Henry J. Allen and with the collapse of
the Kansas Court of Industrial Relations which he had attempted to set up in this State and then sell to the nation
on the theory that workers could be compelled to continue
to work, even when they desired to quit, and that capital
could be forced to operate industries, even at a loss, in order that the general public might have its luxurious essen-
tials. The collapse of this industrial court panacea really
marked the end of political cantankerousness in Kansas—
the end for a time, at least. Conservatism and political apathy spread rapidly as the Allen leadership gave way.

LESS INTEREST IN POLITICS

Today Kansas is less politically minded than ever before in
her history. Campaigns are conducted without the old-
time fireworks displays; the terms "radical" and "conserva-
tist" mean little, either as applied to candidates or causes;
even the Grange, the Farmers' Union and labor organizations do not arouse marked hysteria. To say that Kansans
are less interested in politics because they are occupied with
higher things is a tempting impulse. Also, there is evidence
with which to back up such a statement—evidence of an
increased interest in the arts, music, poetry, painting; evidence of a more tolerant attitude toward opposed ideas,
and a more intelligent inquiry into the enigma of life. More
important still, there is abundant evidence of a more open-
minded inquiry as to the infallibility of present moral
standards. There is some evidence of an increase in the

In the Kansas Senate, from the Balcony, Mary Huntoon

number of individuals who are coming to the view that
richness lies within one's self rather than in one's property
holdings; evangelism which exalts the ego is being
preached in some quarters. A surprising number of hard-
handed farmers know exactly what you mean when you
say that all virtues may be practiced through super-selfish-
ness. But with all these evidences piled on top of the declining interest in political buncombe I am still hesitant to say
that Kansas is leading in the direction of a more elevated
civilization.

Puritanism in its old form, unquestionably, is perishing
along with political claptrappery. Pioneer Kansans were Puritans all the way from the sod house to the Senate Chamber, in spirit as much as, or more than, in lineage. Their
anti-slavery animosities, their ideals, their ideas of equality
and their economic struggles forced them to Puritanical
standards. Out of their Puritanism grew the prohibition
craze which was carried to the point of crusading under
Carry Nation, and which was capitalized for the first time
by the politicians under the leadership of Governor John P.
St. John. Out of prohibition grew the mania for passing
laws to regulate the personal conduct of the individual—
the policy of trying to legislate morality into morons.

No State has gone quite as far in modern times in the en-
actment of laws to regulate private affairs—laws drawn up
for the purpose of improving the individual according to
the majority's idea of improvement. Kansas was the first
State, so far as I can discover, to enact a law regulating the
length of a bed sheet. On the statute books today, in addition to the bone-dry prohibitory laws, there is a law which
forbids the selling or giving away of cigarettes; stringent
anti-gambling enactments which even prohibit punch

boards; a law forbidding an individual who has the inclination to eat snakes, and scores of similar enactments restrictive of personal liberty in matters which should be of no concern to the State. There is a white slavery law which makes it a penitentiary offense for a man to transport a woman across her own front yard for what a jury might decide was an immoral purpose.

A majority of these legal levees have been thrown up as a result of the mental intoxication the prohibition regime brought to the Puritans. Prohibition today is being enforced as effectively as any of these polypus phantasies of popular government. (No one in office in Kansas who expects to run for office again will admit that the anti-drinking laws are not being effectively enforced; no one acquainted with the facts can be honest and say Kansas is as dry as ten years ago.)

The extent to which the hypocrisy and fanaticism brought about by Puritanism and prohibition are undermining the moral fiber of the people cannot be told with accuracy at the present stage. The situation has become such that a man must be either a hypocrite or a fanatic if he hopes for any sort of political preferment. A man of the courage, honesty and ability of Senator James A. Reed of Missouri could not be elected township trustee in any part of Kansas. On every hand officials preach purity and practice law violations with immunity.

OFFICIAL LAW VIOLATORS

For instance, county attorneys and others responsible for enforcing the law buy, smoke and give away cigarettes every day; they commit this offense on the very days they go out

to prosecute drug store proprietors and pool-hall operators 75 KANSAS, ESSENCE OF AMERICA
for violating the anti-cigarette laws. It is the same with the
liquor law enforcement. A large percentage of the population considers it a mark of distinction to be known as liquor law violators and drink regularly; yet, if called upon to
vote on prohibition, they undoubtedly would vote dry.
How much such vices are responsible for fouling the very
nests their perpetrators pretend to feather with angel-wing
down is hard to say. How much the hypocrisy of the public
officials and the public itself is responsible for setbacks to
Puritanism and back-sliding from political progressivism is
a moot question. But, within the last year, the people have
been given some delusion-dispelling, eye-opening incidents
to think about.

The State Supreme Court has actually held that a man's
automobile might be seized, confiscated and sold on the
charge that he had used it in the transportation of liquor
despite the fact that the owner of the car had been acquit-
ted in a jury trial on the charge of having liquor in his possession in the automobile at the time the car was seized.
Within the last year exposure of the Kansas Anti-Saloon
League management proved that the Attorney General of
the State, while drawing the salary of his office also drew a
salary from the Anti-Saloon League, and that while he was
drawing these two salaries the Superintendent of the Anti-
Saloon League also drew money from the State Treasury
for alleged law-enforcement work. Also, it was proved that
a Justice of the State Supreme Court, while receiving his
salary from the State, drew money from the Anti-Saloon
League Treasury, and thousands of dollars was spent by the
Anti-Saloon League on the political campaigns of these officials, while thousands of dollars collected for alleged law-

enforcement work was never used for the purpose intended by those who contributed it.

Is it any wonder Puritanism appears to be declining? When we find public officials and professional uplifters so obtuse to a sense of duty and decency, and so strongly entrenched behind bulwarks of hypocrisy and fanaticism, are we not justified in wondering if the political apathy is induced by an absorption in more inspirational endeavors?

Kansas, nevertheless, has made progress and is making progress along certain lines of cultural development. Her people have become comparatively wealthy: wealth brings leisure and leisure always leads to culture where there are individuals who have tastes, talents, ideals or any form of intelligence. The question is, therefore, Has cultural development kept pace with the opportunities afforded by the fertility of the soil and the development of natural resources; is the Kansas oyster preserving its comfort by producing a beautiful pearl?

Today Kansas produces more hard Winter wheat than any other one State in the world, and nearly one-fifth of all the wheat raised in the United States. This Commonwealth ranks fifth among the States in corn production, third in the production of alfalfa, millet and other cultivated hay crops. From thirty principal farm crops the annual income runs close to $500,000,000. The annual mineral production is estimated by the State Board of Agriculture to be $160,000,000. This same authority in reporting the development of the poultry, egg and dairy industry in May, 1926, said: "In 1925 the farmers of this State sold 16,007,988 dozen eggs more than they sold in 1920. Even at 25 cents a dozen, the average price for all seasons and for the State as a whole, the total of egg production

would represent a value of $23,281,151 for the year, or
$63,784 a day for 365 days. * * * Kansas milk cows in
1925 produced 251,986,977 gallons of milk, which was an
increase of 30,514,560 gallons more than was reported in
the general census year. This is enough milk to fill 50,000
one-hundred barrel cisterns and does not include the
amount produced by town cows."

THE WEALTH OF THE STATE

Live stock products alone bring into the State more than
$100,000,000 a year, and the oil production income runs to
a higher figure. Salt, coal, lead, zinc, clay products and natural gas, lime, asphalt and gypsum bring in many millions
more. And the total population of the State, according to
the 1925 figures, is only 1,833,882. Assessed valuations,
which are always below the real values, show the per capita
wealth is in excess of $2,000. The State's farm lands are val-
ued at $1,729,000,000, personal property is valued at
$696,000,000 and public service corporation property at
$642,000,000.

These figures make a rather imposing showing for a State
that started from scratch less than seventy-five years ago,
with a population made up largely of individuals who had
been unable to hold their heads above water in the surging
streams of civilization in the more thickly populated areas.

No one, surely, would argue that cultural development
has kept pace with this accumulation of wealth; it could
not have been expected. As in all new countries, the people
have been too much occupied with other things. It is
plainly to be seen that the Kansans have been largely engaged in money-making activities. It was not a cultural

urge, but an economic emergency that brought them to the plains to live in sod houses and fight Indians and grasshoppers while trying to establish homes, acquire wealth and set up a Government which would forever guard them and their posterity against becoming under-dogs in a caste-ruled State. They have accomplished these objectives in a most remarkably satisfactory way; they have shown intelligence and efficiency in so doing. The question, therefore, we may ask, is not what the Kansas people have done, but what they are doing, and what they are going to do in the future. It is a most important question because its answer embodies a demonstration of the ability and inclinations of the *great common people*, once their economic problems are solved, to elevate themselves to a higher plane. In Kansas, more than in any other State with which I am familiar, conditions are almost ideal for the demonstration.

Compared with the standards of other States the Kansas schools of today rank high. The public schools are well-manned and the teachers are up to the average in training and intelligence. The higher educational institutions, including Kansas State Agricultural College, at Manhattan, and the State Teachers' Colleges at Pittsburg, Emporia and Hays, are as efficient in turning out standardized mental products as most State institutions. They offer good technical courses, expound majority opinions diplomatically; their students and faculty members make love no more than is common in Kentucky and California institutions.

Strange as it may seem, one of the most encouraging signs comes from the smaller denominational colleges and so-called universities. These institutions always have stood higher than their contemporaries in many other States, and in the last few years they have been moving up rapidly, the best of them squirming out from under the heels of the church and acquiring a freedom which allows them to go about their work in an intelligent fashion. A notable example is Washburn College, a Congregational institution at Topeka. Parley P. Womer, who has been President of this college for a number of years seems to have the knack of picking real teachers for his faculty and convincing them that their talents and intelligence may be used in the classroom. Also, he has administrative ability, which means he keeps the Board of Trustees from meddling with matters beyond their grasp. As a result, his institution is in a healthy state; it has the air of inquisitive freedom and an attitude of liberality.

LITERARY BACKWARDNESS

In the field of literature it seems there is a falling back rather than a going forward, although it may be that the present is only a lounging cat-nap period. With the exception of Edgar Watson Howe, William Allen White and Nelson Antrim Crawford there are no living literati who have won gold spurs and green laureate wreaths. The State has no man or woman of letters to be classed with Sherwood Anderson, Sinclair Lewis, Willa Cather, H. L. Mencken, Ruth Suckow, Ben Hecht, Edna St. Vincent Millay, Carl Sandburg, Ring Lardner, or any of the new school artists who have undertaken the work of entertaining, enlightening and emotionalizing the age. In the matter of verse making Kansas most assuredly has not kept abreast of Oklahoma and Iowa in producing individuals who have followed in the footsteps of Shelley with a willingness to "learn in suffering" that which must be taught "in song."

The largest enterprise for literature in Kansas today is the work of Emanuel Haldeman-Julius of Girard, who is publishing the classics of all ages in ton lots and selling them over the country in the form of his "Little Blue Books" at five cents a copy. His sales, which run into millions, with more than one thousand titles, tell what he is doing in the way of educating the *great common people*. Also, in his monthly and quarterly magazines, through which he has set out on the stupendous work of "de-bunking" America, Haldeman-Julius may be accomplishing more important things than his contemporaries realize.

In the field of journalism the outlook is not as hopeful as it appears on the surface. Kansas has some well-edited small papers. Most of them are prosperous, but, as Henry J. Allen, publisher of the *Wichita Beacon*, recently pointed out, the newspapers of the State do not exert the influence they once did, nor do they enter as aggressively, or as fearlessly, into the making of their communities. Most of them have settled down to money-making. Also, most of the papers that have a circulation large enough to exercise influence are being used by their publishers for personal political aggrandizement.

. . . . .

John G. Neihardt, who permits his admirers to call him the "Homer of the West," recently said that the United States is the only country in the world where lack of culture has developed into a cult. I can hardly hit the nail on the head with such a smashing blow; but, in Mid-America, this seems to be tending toward the real state of affairs. I cannot see that it is any more true in Kansas than it is in Nebraska, New Mexico, or Nevada; but I can see where the charge can be of more national significance if proved against Kansas.

In no part of America has the common man had a better opportunity to demonstrate his ability to rise, to raise himself to a higher plane, economically and socially. In no commonwealth of the United States has the democratic idea been cherished more fondly, or exalted more highly—or made to mean more to the masses. Today in Topeka, the capital city of Kansas, the most exclusive social circles are well sprinkled with the sons and daughters of men who have been section hands on the railroads, sod busters on the prairie and sewer sinkers in the cities. In the list of the State's most recent Governors there are an ex-barber and a former mule-skinner. The most recent ex-Governor, a real "dirt farmer," moved his family into the Executive Mansion from the farm on which he had lived and worked all his life. To the social snob these are not things in which a State may take pride. But in the course of the State's social progress who can say they are not significant signs?

To the critic who would be impatient with Kansas because her cultural development has not seemed to keep pace with her accumulation of wealth, I would ask, Can a social group be expected to change completely in the course of its concentrated energies in a quarter of a century? The critic must remember that Kansas has come into her comparatively wealthy condition at the high tide of our national commercialism, at a time when all the world seems afflicted with a very virulent outbreak of the money mania. Nor must it be forgotten that it is a comparative condition of wealth which the Kansans have attained. The telephone, the radio, the bathtub with running water, electric lights, milking machines and automobiles, with all the costs which go with easy transportation facilities, are now as necessary in maintaining the cherished democratic ideas as a homestead was fifty years ago.

It is not for me to proclaim the relative importance of these things. I cannot prophesy as to the ability of the Kansans to solve their present economic problems and use their energies more intelligently in practicing the art of living. All I can say is that no people are striving more energetically, or with more confidence in themselves and their ideals; and I shall not be surprised if the histories of our era will say: "As Kansas went, so went Democracy."

SKY-MOUNTAIN

May Williams Ward

May Williams Ward, although born in Missouri, attended the University of Kansas where she took a degree in mathematics. She became a serious writer in 1925, at age 43, when she was one of the first Kansans to attend the MacDowell Colony, a prestigious colony for artists, writers, and composers founded in Petersborough, New Hampshire, by the widow of American composer Edward Alexander MacDowell after his death in 1908. She edited The Harp, *one of Kansas' fine poetry magazines, from her home in Belpre for six years. She published six volumes of poetry, often illustrated with her own woodcuts, an autobiography, and numerous book reviews. She died in Wellington, Kansas, which she considered home, in 1975 at the age of 93.*

In its celebration of the landscape, its strict attention to form, and its own spare beauty, "Sky-Mountain" is typical of the fine poetry published in Kansas Magazine, *now* Kansas Quarterly, *published at Kansas State University. The essays by William Inge, Peg Wherry, William Least Heat-Moon, and Denise Low all echo Ward's satisfaction with a wide landscape that creates mountains inside.*

MAY
WILLIAMS
WARD

Prairie-land is golden,
Airy, wide;

The sky our only mountain;
We, inside.

Who would choose a small land
Where the hills

Steadily asserting
Granite wills,

Narrow all horizons,
Stand apart?

Ah, my Kansas prairie
In the sky-mountain's heart!

1927

Kansas Farm in Winter, Arthur W. Hall

BLEEDING KANSANS

Karl A. Menninger

Karl Augustus Menninger, known to most Kansans as "Dr. Karl," was born of pioneer Kansas parents in 1893 near Topeka. He was educated at Washburn University, the University of Wisconsin, and the Harvard University Medical School. He returned to Kansas and, joined by his father and brothers, founded the Menninger Clinic in a farmhouse just outside Topeka in 1925. The clinic grew into the present Menninger and now trains doctors from all over the world in psychiatry and psychoanalysis. Menninger's ideas about therapeutic treatment helped change both public institutions for, and attitudes toward, the mentally ill. Menninger's books include The Human Mind *(1930),* Man against Himself *(1938), and more recently,* Whatever Became of Sin? *(1973). Karl Menninger died on 18 July 1990, just four days before his ninety-seventh birthday.*

In "Bleeding Kansans," Menninger takes on the characteristic "self-depreciation" of Kansans toward themselves and their state. Though he chastises Kansans for being ashamed of anything but their joyless asceticism, he writes affectionately of Kansas traditions, beauty, and high spiritual ideals. In fact, he shows how these great ideals and great historical struggles work against positive feelings: How can Kansans help but feel self-deprecatory when they have such heights to live up to and are so bound to fail? Menninger's words must have spoken elo-

quently to Kansans of 1939, who were just recovering from years of economic depression and drought, and who saw themselves portrayed in The Wizard of Oz *(released in 1939) as joyless, driven, and hard-bitten. His words live today as Kansans and Midwesterners struggle for a positive identity against images bestowed by Hollywood and New York (and, Menninger would say, by ourselves). And we still risk becoming either reclusive (William Stafford's poem begins "Mine was a Midwestern home; you can keep your world") or noisily eccentric (Robert Day mines this material effectively in "Not in Kansas Anymore").*

Sometimes when I have just returned from the mountains or the seashore, friends who meet me on the street exclaim sympathetically but enviously about my trip: "Were you not sorry to leave?" They ask, "Isn't it hard to come back from such beautiful places into the drab monotony of our Kansas scenery?"

When they say such things I cannot answer them; I cannot even look at them for fear of betraying my thoughts. I look at the ground or I look past them to the horizon. Inwardly I recall the words of a famous Kansan who wrote to his wife on December 10, 1854:

"... Our food is mush, molasses and bacon, mixed plentifully with dirt three times each day. Thus we live in Kansas. *A more lovely country I certainly never saw—* and yet it looks worse now than at any other season. I am told by those who know that in the spring and early summer when the grass and shrubbery and flowers appear it is beautiful beyond conception. So I think it must be. And in a few years when civilization by its magic influence shall have transformed this glorious country from what it now is to the brilliant destiny awaiting it, the sun in all his course will visit *no land more truly lovely and desirable than this . . . .*"*

This man was one of the truly great Kansans because he had vision, a vision not only for the future, but for the present realities. And he had come to Kansas from one of the most beautiful states in the union, Pennsylvania.

I am well aware that the other side of the road looks smoother and the grass in the opposite field greener, but I believe this inability of some Kansans to appreciate their own state has a far deeper psychological origin. It is observable in so many different ways. I have sometimes called it, in our professional jargon, a characteristic feeling of inferiority. We seem to share it with the state of Arkansas which is also a beautiful and creditable state, but whose citizens are often ashamed of having originated there. I see the self-depreciation of Kansans exhibiting itself in the form of a sense of uneasiness, an apologetic manner when in the association of the representatives of older and wealthier states, and in a tendency to join with them in a bantering ridicule of our state instead of recognizing how much this represents a defense of their own ignorant provincialism. But more serious, I think, is a kind of asceticism, a willingness to accept as our fate and lot a far less comfortable and joyous existence than could be ours almost for the asking. This, too, springs from our self-depreciation.

No one could ask for a better illustration of this than the prohibition sentiment of the state. I know, as everyone else

*See "Letters of Cyrus Kurtz Holliday, 1854–1859," edited by Lela Barnes, *Kansas Historical Quarterly* 6(1937):246.

knows, that there are relatively few total abstainers in Kansas, but to keep up appearances we must not buy or sell liquor publicly. We must smuggle it in from Missouri to the cynical but gratified amusement of our less hypocritical eastern neighbors. We comfort ourselves with the logic that because some men are fools all men must be martyrs. The fact that there may be joy in wine is forgotten in the face of the fact that there may be tears in rum. Kansans have no sense of superiority about their prohibition. Some comfort themselves with a puritanical sense of self-righteousness, but it is cold comfort. For the same energies that have prohibited the open sale of liquor would have gone much further had they been invested in the promotion of beauty, the improvement of highways, the enlargement of parks, the fostering of music and art.

Not but what we have done fairly well with music and art. I am proud of what we have done. But I am afraid that most of my fellow Kansans are not. They are not proud of it because they realize that it is so much less than we could have done had we not had an ascetic disapproval of joy or anything that would make it appear that we were a happy, progressive, successful state. We want to be "bleeding Kansas." When someone calls us a typical prairie state we get angry, not because we think we have been misunderstood but because we fear we have been understood too well and our shame publicly exposed.

I would be happy to believe that our feelings of inferiority are only the expression of an innate modesty, a feeling of revulsion against the flamboyant, bombastic egotism of California and the similar arrogance of a few other states. Unfortunately I cannot believe this. Kansas does not refrain from announcing that it has the best of this or the best of that because of our essential good taste; Kansas does not announce it because Kansas does not believe it. When I tell friends that I think our scenery is beautiful and that our climate is delightful (Cyrus Holliday said that it was better than that of sunny Italy) my friends think that I am ironic or a little "touched." They would much rather read in the paper that we had broken a heat record so that they could use it to prove their martyrdom than to reflect that hot weather is the healthiest weather of all and that fewer people die from the effects of the climate in Kansas than in almost any other state. Yesterday it was 97 in Los Angeles; it was 70 in Topeka. But I am sure this fact was not headlined by any Kansas newspapers, and I am more certain that it was not headlined by any California papers. Last week New England was ravaged by a terrific wind storm which did more damage in one hour than all the tornadoes have done in Kansas since the dawn of civilized history, but I am sure that this was not noted by any Kansas newspapers nor by any of the eastern newspapers which still play up "Kansas cyclones."

Not long ago the son of a colleague came to me for advice in regard to entering my Alma Mater, the Harvard Medical School. He was afraid that he would not be admitted. I remarked that the fact that he was a Kansan would probably be to his advantage in his consideration by the committee. "Well," he exclaimed, "that will be the first time that coming from Kansas ever did me any good!" I could not think of any reply to this. He was a handsome young fellow, a member of the third generation since the pioneers. His family has prospered (in Kansas!) and he was as nattily dressed, as sophisticated in manner as the boys I have known from Harvard and Hopkins, and Pennsylvania. But the poor fellow does not know it. He labors under a sense of inferiority which is pitiful. He goes to college with a sensitiveness which will probably make him either a recluse or a noisy eccentric.

I am fairly familiar with the physicians of America, and I can honestly say that I believe that we have within the confines of our state medical men quite as capable as those in most other comparable localities. Ambitiously we endeavor to maintain a medical school, but we do not trust it to be staffed by Kansas doctors. The students of the medical school of the University of Kansas are instructed by men borrowed from Missouri, Missouri doctors from Kansas City.

The phenomenon of the city of "Kansas City, Missouri," is perhaps the most brilliant illustration of my thesis. Poor Kansas City is an orphan town; it has no parent state. Missouri disowns it as a metropolis; St. Louis is the Missouri city, and Kansas City should be the Kansas city, but it isn't. Rather, it is and it isn't. It is located largely in Missouri, populated largely with ex-Kansans, depends upon Kansas for its economic existence, supplies Kansas with traveling salesmen, truckdrivers, and racketeers, instructs Kansans how to vote and considers Kansas its great backyard. Kansans, none the less, think it is a great metropolis and speak of it reverently as "the city."

Think of a state smart enough to issue a Magazine [*Kansas Magazine*] like this one! Think of a state with people wise enough to abolish capital punishment fifty years ago. Think of a state with people in it capable of erecting a structure like the Santa Fe Railroad or an organization like the Capper press. Think of a state with a Historical Society such as ours. We have heard a lot about wheat, but con-

Sunshine Creek, Birger Sandzen

sider the trees; we are the only state in the union without a national forest, and yet we are also the only state in the union with more trees in it than at the time it was settled. Think of a state with people in it like William Allen White and Ed Howe and Nelson Antrim Crawford, Howard Carruth and Esther Clark, John James Ingalls, Charles M. Sheldon, Kirke Mechem, and W. G. Clugston, Birger Sandzen, and many others. You know this is not a state of mediocrities. The same humility of spirit is to be observed in the Kansas intellectuals, in the Kansas voters, and the Kansas press. In their eagerness to be broadminded, tolerant, democratic, they have listened receptively to many prophets, some false, some true, and have followed them fervently. This fervent response—a response sometimes bordering on fanaticism—is regarded by many easterners as characteristic of the people of Kansas. In abolition, prohibition, Populism, anti-tobacco legislation, Brinkley worship, Winrodism, etc., they have gone off the deep end with desperate seriousness, and in so doing earned for themselves the name of being a humorless, puritanical people, incapable of joy and grudging in their attitude toward those happier than themselves.

This is not a pretty reputation and naturally one shrinks from accepting this description of oneself and his friends and neighbors. Oddly enough, however, we do accept it almost unanimously and meekly endure the opprobrium and ridicule of other states. This I believe to be due to a humility and self-distrust so great as to be crippling to our energies.

For the fanaticism of Kansans is due, I believe, not so much to puritanical self-righteousness, the desire to reform and inhibit, as it is to a wish to identify themselves with the best, the most idealistic and fruitful ways of life. And because they feel pathetically unequal to maintaining these ideals and to living at the high pitch at which they conceive other more gifted people to be living, they fence themselves about and reinforce their tense strivings with laws and prohibitions.

In discussing Kansans it is usually assumed that their strictness is aimed at coercing other people to their beliefs, to reform the wicked. The reformer's psychology is often described as being a desire to keep others from the sinful pleasures he secretly indulges in or at least burns to indulge in. This unsympathetic portrayal of the reformer as a hypocrite and a dog in the manger has some truth in it; but this very intolerance of the intolerant betrays an unconscious hypocrisy in the hypocrite-hater. To put away the temptation to indulge in more paradoxical but perhaps confusing expressions, let us state it more plainly by saying that at heart everyone is a reformer in the sense that he must curb certain anti-social tendencies in himself which he openly deprecates but yearns to indulge. We say that his attitudes are unconscious because he is not aware of such yearnings and would probably develop all kinds of defensive symptoms if he began to be aware of the strength of unlawful desires in himself. The activities of the zealot who rushes about making life miserable for other people may be considered as one form of defensive symptom of this type. His activity therefore is chiefly directed against himself, in spite of its apparent direction toward the world in general. The world may avoid him, trip him up, laugh at him, and find many ways of overcoming the discomfort he causes, but he has no way of circumventing his own unrelenting harshness toward himself which drives him to take desperate measures to reinforce his failing defense against anti-social urges.

I began by saying that we live in a beautiful state, a state settled by brave, intelligent and far-visioned people; then I had to add that our intelligence and our vision do not seem to have prevented us from developing a vast inferiority, not a real inferiority but a feeling of inferiority. I related this inferiority to feelings of over-conscientiousness which in turn I think may be an echo of the pioneer struggles of our immediate ancestors. We need writers and artists to proclaim the beauty of Kansas and to demonstrate the intelligence of the majority and not the eccentricity of the lunatic fringe.

The members of the press have a special responsibility in this matter. I have long felt that the newspapers could modify the unfavorable opinions of the outsiders if they would modify the feelings of Kansans about themselves. For the men of the press reflect this attitude of inferiority; indeed they encourage it; they exploit it. They like to brag about breaking heat records and raising freaks. They feel a little shamefaced in writing about our cultural attainments. The newspaper reporters seem to feel impelled to pull a wisecrack if possible, and the desk man would rather think up a funny headline than an accurate one. They deceive themselves into thinking the people like this. The truth of the matter is that too many of the newspaper men do not take their own work seriously. They do not take their state seriously. If the Wichita newspapers, for example, would give more space to the glories of Kansas and less to the iniquities of Topeka; if the Topeka newspapers would give more space to the cultural activities of the city and less to the political goings-on in the State House, and if all the editors of all the papers would read the *Kansas Magazine* and print excerpts from it instead of lifting paragraphs from the Kansas City Star, we would have an even better state than we have now, and we would have more fun living in it or visiting outside of it.

THE COTTONWOOD
AND THE PRAIRIE

Zula Bennington Greene

Zula Bennington Greene was best known as "Peggy of the Flint Hills," the name she took for her newspaper column, begun for the Chase County Leader-News in 1928. Born in Missouri, raised and educated in Colorado, she moved with her new husband to Chase County, near Bazaar, when she was in her twenties. In 1933, when she moved to Topeka, she began writing for the Topeka Daily Capital (later the Topeka Capital-Journal). In 1983, she celebrated fifty years of six columns per week, over fifteen thousand altogether; the best of them appear in her book, Skimming the Cream (1983). Peggy Greene's work is full of insight, humor, and a sense of beauty. As William Allen White said of her: "A pair of eyes like Peggy has is worth far more than a college education or a trip around the world. She can get more out of life staying at home than most people can from traveling." In the two pieces printed below, Greene describes cottonwoods and prairies, two things often contemplated by Kansans who stay at home.

The cottonwood is not a sturdy or long-lived tree, like the oak. Its wood is not valued, like the walnut's. It does not even make good firewood. But it has an airy grace that pays its way.

Cottonwoods, Arthur W. Hall

The early settlers planted the cottonwood around their houses because it was quick-growing. Its frilly daintiness must have warmed the heart of the pioneer woman and its soft rustle whispered to her of courage and faith.

Through the heat of the summer it stands cool and clean and shining. The leaves shake off dust as nervously as a fluttery housewife polishes the furniture, never content to sit a moment with quiet hands. In the night it makes a rain-sound on the roof.

The cotton is a sympathetic tree, sensitive, brooding, like those yearning souls who love to bear burdens. It sighs its distress that man's progress through this vale of tears should be so vexing.

But it never intrudes. It expresses its feeling in well-bred murmurs. It asks no questions, but tenderly flutters down its leaves. They fall as easily and copiously as a woman's tears, which, blotted and wiped away, start falling again with each new sigh.

A cottonwood is a tree to live with. I'm sure it is good luck to have it bless the hearth with a baptism of leaves for the first fire.

* * * * *

The prairies do not startle you with sudden vivid beauty as a turn in a mountain road can do. They do not dazzle you or exhaust you with excitement. There are no dramatic tricks. They are a quality rather than a quantity.

They are as patient as time and as mysterious as the stars. They are a woman who is neither beautiful nor brilliant, clever nor accomplished. At first you scarcely notice her as she moves silent and serene and unadorned.

Afterwards in a quiet moment she walks into your mind. There is the sound of her voice, the movement of her hand, the peace in her eyes, and more than these—a strange rare essence of earthiness you can never forget.

Ignore her—she is calm and sufficient. Shut her out of your sight—there she is again beyond the little town with awnings flapping in the breeze and the next town and the next, with as many moods as the wind, drawing you on.

She is not the gorgeous woman you dreamed should some day be yours, but she is mystery and tenderness and strength and rapture, and suddenly you know that this is what you wanted all of your life.

100

ZULA
BENNINGTON
GREENE

The knowledge comes as gently as the prairie dusk. You sigh in peaceful surrender.

ADDRESS TO KANSANS

Kenneth Wiggins Porter

*Although Kenneth Wiggins Porter (1905–1981) is best known
for his long and distinguished career as a historian, which he
pursued outside Kansas, his second love, for poetry, mined almost exclusively Kansas material, and resulted in many insight-
ful, humorous, historically analytical, and politically oriented
poems about the state. Born in Sterling, Porter was educated at
Sterling College, the University of Minnesota, and Harvard
University. During the Great Depression, he returned to Sterling, broke, and his historical, political and poetic visions came
together. His two books of poetry,* The High Plains *(1938) and*
No Rain From These Clouds *(1946), still contain the best
poems to come out of the Kansas experience of the Dirty Thirties. "Address to Kansans" is the first of a series of poems,
titled "Ad Astra Per Aspera," that Porter wrote at the request
of William Allen White for the dedication of the Municipal
Auditorium, Emporia.*

Here was no 'stern and rockbound coast,'
no 'forest primeval,'
no 'rocks and rills' nor 'woods and templed hills'
to love;
but an ocean of grass to the stirrups;
river 'half a mile wide and half an inch deep'—
or five miles by twenty feet

at the time of spring rains in the mountains;
hills were outcroppings of rock—
knobs on the backs of great saurians.
Here no romantic tradition-hallowed forest-dangers—
the tall dark brooding trees
leaning soul-crushingly inward;
the panther on the bough;
snuffle of wolves at the door-cranny:
instead
the horizon dragging outward at the heart-walls;
the land drought-crucified
the hosts of tiny vicious flying dragons;
the screaming down-rush of the white-hooded three day
   blizzard;
the ocean of grass a stormy sea of flame.
Many came to this land
and some stayed.
As for those who did not,
God grant that they found greener pastures.
As for those who dug in and survived,
their names are familiar to you,
are your own, in whole or in part,
the names of your children.

1946

Farm Animals in a Flood, John Steuart Curry

THE STRENGTH OF KANSAS

Milton S. Eisenhower

Milton S. Eisenhower (1899–1985) was born in Abilene and educated at what is now Kansas State University. He was a teacher, director of information for the U.S. Department of Agriculture (1928–1941), and director of the War Relocation Authority (1941–1943) before resigning to become president of Kansas State University. In 1950, he became president of Pennsylvania State College, and from 1956 until his retirement he was president of Johns Hopkins University. He served often in diplomatic positions during the administrations of Harry Truman and his brother, Dwight David Eisenhower.

Eisenhower's "The Strength of Kansas" appropriately joins to the Puritan heritage of Kansas the southern cultural traditions which went underground during the Civil War but surfaced in the chivalric, assertive, highly individualistic Texas cowboy and later rancher and oil driller of western Kansas, a place where even after the settlement of the frontier, southern traits helped Kansans thrive in a speculative, high-risk economy. Eisenhower maintains that the "hybrid vigor" of Kansas, though weakened after leading the country between 1860 and 1920, has rested long enough (thirty years). Kansas, he says, is the center, the heart, of all that is American: Puritan and southern; urban and rural; agricultural and industrial; in the middle of a country that must face outward to both Europe and China. Eisenhower outlines a big task in his conclusion, but uses his own life as example: if only Kansas can do what he did, apply Kansas values to wider horizons, we will lead again, restored to our rightful place as a state vital to the Union and the world. Some of his sentiments are echoed just five years later as Allan Nevins looks at Kansas' place in American history.

It is a rough approximation of the truth to say that two distinctive cultures have met in Kansas to shape the unique spirit of our people. If the spirit has been a turbulent one in the past, and if the turbulence has been creative, it is because the two cultures which met here were in many respects antagonistic to one another: Their marriage produced that vital phenomenon which the artist calls "dramatic conflict" and which the plant breeder calls "hybrid vigor."

The first wave of Kansas settlement was swept into the eastern part of the State on the historic tide whose crest was the Civil War. By and large, the leaders of the Kansas immigrants in the late 1850's were New England men of conscience; they were Abolitionists. Raised in the Puritan tradition, fired by the courage of strong convictions, they were armed spiritually and physically for the righteous war. Their respect for human personality had, as its counterpart, a passionate hatred for slavery.

But the personality they respected was bound by iron commitments to a stern God. Thus the very strength of their convictions, driving them to battle for Negro freedom, inclined them toward intolerance of moral conceptions which differed from theirs. The freedom they claimed for themselves and fought to obtain for others, was hedged about by prohibitions. Sometimes those prohibitions were extended to innocent, pleasurable acts simply because they were pleasurable.

However, these early settlers were men and women of whom their descendants may be justly proud. The marks they left upon our state were for the most part good marks. They were virile people, strong people, brave people. They had vision and integrity. They had a profound moral concern which is too much gone from our modern world, and—far from being the dull stodgy folk pictured by their enemies—they had the zeal of radical reformers.

In the late 1860's and the 1870's, this Kansas Puritan tradition was reinforced by an influx of Swedish Lutherans, German-Russian Mennonites, and so-called Pennsylvania Dutch belonging to those Mennonite sects known as Dunkards and River Brethren. A large colony of the latter— River Brethren—settled in Dickinson County in 1878. Among them were my grandfather and father.

But this Puritan culture was not the only one to be transplanted to Kansas. From the first, it was confronted by a culture alien to it and even antagonistic. Though New England Abolitionists made up the bulk of the first settlement, they came, it must be remembered, because pro-slavery Southerners were also coming in considerable numbers—and these Southerners were different from the New England people in several important respects.

To list these differences is to risk the fallacy of oversimplification. Nevertheless, a large measure of truth can be expressed by saying that the democratic principle, associated with freedom of economic enterprise, animated the New Englander, whereas the aristocratic principle, associated with a feudal stratification of society from slave to manor lord, determined the manners and morals of the South.

It follows that warfare, an unpleasant duty for the Puritan New Englander, was often a glorious adventure to the Southern Cavalier. Martial valor was deemed a value by the New Englander only when it was guided by a moral intention. No such scruple inhibited the admiration aroused, in Southern breasts, by brave deeds and braver words. To many a Southerner battle courage was, in and of itself, a supreme value.

Temperamental differences between North and South were reflected in the very songs of the pioneer Kansan. New England settlers interspersed old Puritan hymns with such lugubrious secular ballads as "Empty is the Cradle," and "Willie Has Gone With the Angels." Settlers from the South, on the other hand, sang few hymns at their social get-togethers. Instead they sang gay sentimental songs like "Sweet Violets, Fairer Than All the Roses," and "The Yellow Rose of Texas Beats the Belle of Tennessee."

Thus was the New Englander innately suspicious of worldly pleasures, whereas the Southerner carelessly embraced them. The New Englander aimed to be virtuous, the Southerner aimed to be gallant, and the not too humble piety professed by the Puritan was likely to present itself to the Cavalier as a contemptible hypocrisy.

In the years of "Bleeding Kansas," the exponents of these two cultures struggled bitterly for possession of the Kansas Territory. The defeat of the Southerners was final and crushing. Eighty-eight years ago the House of Representatives passed the bill admitting Kansas to the Union (the bill having been approved by the Senate seven days before). By that time civil strife had determined that the settled eastern end of our State was to be in its earliest years a transplanted New England.

But the defeat of the Southerners did not mean the extinction, in Kansas, of their fighting and gaming values, their traditions of gallant gesture and dashing courage. Indeed, these latter, submerged by Puritanism east of Manhattan, were dominant forces a few miles farther west.

For here, during almost two decades following the Civil War, was America's wild western frontier. Here were the vast plains of buffalo hunts and Indian wars, of cattle trails and wild cow towns: Abilene, Wichita, Hays, Dodge City. Here was the land of the Western scout, the Plainsman, the Cowboy come up from Texas on the Chisholm Trail. These men were much more inclined toward the Southerner's fighting chivalry and gambling instincts than toward the New Englander's piety.

The man of the frontier took his pleasures where he found them. He was impatient of legality, and all too willing to make his own law (and enforce it, too) with a six gun. His ideal person was compounded, not of piety and moral goodness, but of physical toughness, skillfulness with animals and weapons, an assertive independence, and the kind of courage known as "cold nerve." He was, indeed, a rugged individualist.

Nor did this frontier culture die out completely as the frontier itself disappeared in the 1880's and '90's. Rather it became, in a sense, the vital core of the Kansas which developed west of Salina. The economy of western Kansas— the land of wheat, and oil, and cattle—has necessarily been a speculative one.

Thus, in a precarious land, elements of the frontier spirit—the values of endurance, of courage, of willingness to take a chance—were encouraged to maintain themselves in full vigor, and they have done so to this day.

The interaction of these different cultures—the friction between New England and the South, between Puritanism and the Wild West: each modifying the other, checking the other, stimulating the other—the interaction of these produced, I think, the distinctive Kansas spirit. As I've said, the spirit has displayed, in the past, a good deal of "hybrid vigor." During the first half-century of the state's existence, it manifested itself in a number of strong vivid personalities who spread abroad a picture of Kansas far different from that which prevails today. Some of them were personalities whose morals were dubious but whose color and energy were beyond question—people like John Brown, Jim Lane, John J. Ingalls, Sockless Jerry Simpson, Mary Ellen Lease, Carry Nation, Ed Howe and William Allen White. They stood for something, these people. They were sharply-defined characters who were legendary in their own day and about whom legends still cluster. They made things happen in Kansas.

It would have occurred to no one to call Kansas complacent or commonplace in the years from 1860 to about 1915. On the contrary, Kansas was known as among the most progressive of all states, high-minded, quick to react to needs, a leader in a dozen forms of social legislation. It was Kansas which tackled the liquor interests and defeated them at a time when liquor was among the most powerful, corrupting influences in politics. When we adopted Prohibition in 1881—the second state in the Union to do so—the legislation was bold and progressive.

It was Kansas which tackled the railroads and defeated them at a time when railroads were at the height of their arrogant power and had many state governments in their pockets. When a board of railroad commissioners was es-

tablished in 1883 with authority to fix freight and passen-
ger rates and regulate working conditions, there were loud
cries of "radicalism." It was Kansas which helped lead the
way in 1889 with an eight-hour labor law and with laws establishing compulsory education, limiting child labor, setting up a juvenile court, and establishing standards for san-
itation for the packing and other industries. Kansas's "blue
sky" law, regulating and supervising investment compan-
ies, became model legislation for a score of other states.
When Kansas extended complete suffrage to women in
1913, only six other states, none of them lying east of us,
had already done so.

No, there was nothing complacent about the Kansas of
those years. As late as 1922, William Allen White could
proclaim with typical White exuberance that when anything was going to happen in this country, it happened first
in Kansas. Wrote he: "Abolition, Prohibition, Populism,
and Bull Moose, the exit of roller towel, the appearance of
the bank guarantee, the blue sky law . . . these things come
popping out in Kansas like bats out of hell. Sooner or later
other states take up these things, and then Kansas goes on
breeding other troubles."

White concluded his editorial with that challenging war-
whoop so characteristic of his compositions. "Kansas, fair,
fat, and sixty-one last month," he wrote, "is the nation's
tenth muse, the muse of prophecy. There is just one way to
stop progress in America; and that is to hire some hungry
earthquake to come along and gobble up Kansas."

But when White wrote these lines he was looking backward. The Kansas of his vivid description was not the Kansas of 1922, and certainly not the Kansas of the following
two decades. It was rather a Kansas which had begun to

fade into historic memory with the passing of the Bull Moose in 1912. For the Bull Moose seemed to be the last big upsurge of that energy which had made Kansas a bold breaker of new ground. I'm not saying that the old fire died, but it ceased to flame, it ceased to light up the Kansas scene. It smouldered in the background and cast off sparks, now and then—sparks which fell, however, on no combustible material.

Five decades of epic poetry were followed by three decades of pedestrian prose. The warriors of freedom, the crusaders for righteousness, the fighting visionaries—these ceased to set the tone for Kansas. They yielded their mantles of leadership. A complacency strange to Kansas tended to smother honest criticism and discourage creative genius. Kansas lost its distinction as a social barometer for the nation, an exciting idea and a prophecy. She became simply one of the midland states.

Kansas leaders in industry, trade, education, and politics were no longer distinguishable from those of other Middle Western states. Kansas journalism, once remarkable for its vigor and quality, declined—with one or two notable exceptions—to the level of average journalism throughout the country. Kansas art and literature, though they gained in intrinsic power and quality, were no longer recognized as distinctively Kansan and were certainly no longer objects of state pride. Indeed one of the greatest of Kansas artists, John Steuart Curry, was actually an object of ridicule when, in the 1930's, he was at work on his world-famous mural in our Capitol. He was so badly hurt thereby that he failed to complete his project. He went back to Wisconsin where the State University had been proud to make him its painter-in-residence.

Self, John Steuart Curry

What had happened to Kansas? Plant breeders have found that hybrid vigor fades out a generation or two after the initial cross. Is that what had happened to Kansas?

William Allen White asked similar questions. He, who had written such lusty boasts about his native state in 1922, was writing in a wholly different vein in 1934. In an article entitled "Just Wondering," White asked where Kansas had lost its vitality, why Kansas no longer produced "rugged Shakespearean characters," why Kansans failed to take pride in the art of Birger Sandzen as they had once taken pride in the oratory of Ingalls.

"Times change," concluded White, "and men change with them, but where in our hearts is the blood that begot us?"

Where is it?

I think that the blood which begot us flows undiminished through our hearts, nourishing a basic strength that is still unimpaired. The difficulty has been not that Kansas lost her vitality, but that she lost her sense of direction. In consequence the state's still remarkable energies have been spent too often upon issues which are no longer of central importance in a world struggling to organize itself for the atomic age. It is as though a huge tractor, badly needed for plowing acres of wheatland, were being used to plow and replow a kitchen garden.

And how did this happen? Why did it happen?

Let me try to answer these questions, first, in terms of Kansas experience and, second, in terms of my own personal experience, which parallels that of Kansas in many ways.

The Kansas experience begins with the first white men to enter the Kansas Territory. They were wilderness men:

hunters, trappers and explorers, completely self-reliant and
having few relationships with other people. They need acknowledge no permanent allegiance to anyone other than themselves. Then came the colonist, and these necessarily felt an intense allegiance to their colonies. Each man came to identify himself with his town and his community, but (and this is important) he did so without sacrificing any of his allegiance to his family or his own inner being. He simply expanded his selfhood, his area of self-identification, considerably beyond those of the wilderness man.

Soon settlements were more closely bound together by highways and railroads, by laws and customs, under the aegis of Kansas government, and state pride was born—a still larger selfhood, a still larger area of self-identification—but again without sacrifice of allegiance to self and family and community.

But various factors kept Kansas from industrializing and urbanizing as rapidly as the country as a whole was doing. The country, in the twentieth century, began to wrestle with problems which seemed foreign to our rural experience: problems of industrial relations, monopoly, corporate taxation, and so on. This meant that issues which were part of the concrete daily experience of millions of Americans could be grasped by the average Kansan only through an effort of imagination, supported by a study of distant evidence and abstractions.

Naturally many of us failed to grasp them. Industrialization, intense specialization, impersonality in work, the rise of slum-infested cities—these were profoundly affecting the lives of men in other areas, and we, quite naturally, failed for a time to comprehend. The result was that the Kansas voice ceased to command national attention as it formerly had done. We began to be spoken of as isolationists without large program or purposeful idea. Our once-glorious and creative state pride degenerated into a half-ashamed provincialism.

In other words, the tendency toward an enlarged self-identification, toward a wider, more inclusive, and more effective allegiance, had become temporarily blocked in Kansas. For the time being, we failed to see that an objective understanding of and personal identification with all significant national and international affairs were not only vitally necessary, but could be achieved without loss of cherished allegiances to state, community, and family.

My own experience, as I've said, parallels and so illustrates that of Kansas. My own first vital allegiance was, of course, to my family which was remarkably close-knit and self-sufficient. We raised nearly all our own food. For example, we repaired our own shelter and we made our own amusements. There was no felt need for me to identify myself, in my earliest childhood, with a social area beyond home and family.

But when I went to school I immediately entered upon a wider area of allegiance. I identified myself with the Abilene community. It was still, in many aspects, a frontier community, with a frontier sense of self-sufficiency. There was then no conception of that exacting economic interdependence which now conditions all our lives. Most farmers worked in the certain knowledge that their economic welfare would be determined solely by the efficiency of their handiwork and the behavior of the weather. The fence line was their economic horizon. Most businessmen worked in the certain knowledge that their own enterprise was the sole determinant of their success or failure. Their economic

horizon was the boundary of the Abilene trade territory.
And certainly I did not identify this community in any vital way with state, national, or world movements. When I
heard about the Russo-Japanese war, I felt only such emotions as were aroused by a good Western pulp story.

But when I became a college student and drilled with the
S.A.T.C. in the closing months of World War I, my area of
self-identification was abruptly enlarged. I began to identify
myself with the problems of Kansas and, less vividly, with
those of the United States. I began to see that some of my
earlier attitudes had been narrowly limited, that the world
was both larger and more complicated than I had imag-
ined. Indeed, this world seemed, in some of its aspects, actually terrifying to me when, upon my graduation, I was
suddenly plunged deep into its problems. First in Scotland,
then in Washington, D.C., I was required to identify myself
personally with problems far outside any area of allegiance
I had known before. I was, for a time, bewildered by the
novelty and complexity of these problems. I felt insecure
and inadequate.

But I did, as the months passed, learn to identify myself
with the larger, more complex world in which I must live
and work. I found a new sense of direction, and a new satisfaction in the performance of the tasks assigned to me.
And I did so without loss of my earlier allegiances to family, and town, and state. Rather these earlier allegiances
were expanded and enhanced in value—for certain virtues
and traditions I'd taken for granted in Abilene, Kansas, became unique sources of strength in Washington, D.C. This
value has been still further enhanced for me as, in recent
years, I have joined with educational leaders in many other

countries in an effort to build the moral and intellectual solidarity of mankind.

Thus does my personal history illustrate in a very simple way, I think, the course Kansas has taken to her present position, though in the case of Kansas the loss of direction may have been one aspect of a well-earned rest. After all, Kansas might well have needed rest, having passed a certain number of miracles, and conquered some few mountains of obstacles, during the first six decades of her existence. But now, I am convinced, the period of rest is over. A giant, awakened by the war just ended, is stirring in our earth. Kansas is recovering her sense of direction. Everywhere I see evidences that individual citizens of our state are widening their horizons, expanding the area of their allegiance, bringing to bear upon national and world problems certain values and energies which are uniquely Kansan.

I summed up this evidence in my mind on a homeward journey from Lebanon.

Because I was returning from a UNESCO Conference, I thought of the Kansas response to UNESCO—the most energetic and intelligent response yet made by any similar region in the world. All over Kansas—in schools, colleges, discussion groups, civic clubs, county and State UNESCO organizations—individual Kansans are working hard to build, in their own minds, that sympathetic understanding of other peoples which is one of the indispensable conditions of peace. This fact alone is enough to remove completely from Kansas the stigma of complacency and isolationism.

Because I was returning from an impoverished area, poor in natural resources and deficient in industry, I thought of the economic arrangements which peace requires—and here again the Kansas response has been heartening. Kansans give firm support to the European recovery program, because they realize that Fascism and Communism feed on mass misery and despair, and I see encouraging evidence that Kansans are thinking beyond the Marshall Plan. They anticipate the establishment, through the United Nations, of world trade agreements and of many other kinds of close economic cooperation among the nations, for they realize that only through such cooperation can world problems of soil conservation, of nutrition, of atomic energy, of health, be solved—problems whose solution is essential to the very survival of civilization.

Moreover Kansans, during the recent campaign, displayed increased awareness that foreign policy and domestic program are inseparably linked, so that our actions regarding inflation, monopoly, agricultural economy, civil liberties—all these have foreign policy implications. The United States of America is now the Atlas of the free world. We must for the time being support that world upon our shoulders—until it is strong enough to walk with us on the path of peace.

And Kansas is the heart of the Atlas! Herein lies our state's great strength, her opportunity to serve mankind. Geographically and spiritually, Kansas is at the heart of our continental power.

We are balanced halfway between the America facing Europe and the America facing China. We are that happy mixture of town and country, agriculture and industry, which seems best suited to the maintenance of democratic attitudes. We have a state spirit which is a unique mingling of Puritan morality, Southern chivalry, and Western indi-

A Kansas Wheatfield, Herschel C. Logan

vidualism. No state is more accurately representative of America as a whole than Kansas, and none is placed in a more decisive strategic position.

Thus the awakening of Kansas, the rising up of this giant in the earth, has a hopeful significance for the world we believe in. Sacrificing none of her devotion to political and intellectual freedom, nor to democratic concepts of human dignity and equality, nor to the Christian principle of mutuality in human relations, nor to the conviction that private competitive enterprise yields greater rewards than any other system devised by men—sacrificing none of these, I say, Kansas is now ready to serve as the sane moderator of ideological extremes, the firm core of the American culture and the vital center of creative compromise.

KANSAS AND
THE STREAM OF
AMERICAN DESTINY

Allan Nevins

Allan Nevins (1890–1971) was one of the most prominent historians of the Civil War, as well as a Pulitzer Prize–winning biographer. Born in Illinois, he was educated at the University of Illinois (M.A., 1914). Nevins pursued a journalism career until 1928, when he joined the faculty at Columbia University, where he started the first oral history program in the United States. He retired in 1958 to become senior research associate of Huntington Library.

Invited to give an address at the University of Kansas in celebration of Kansas' territorial centennial in 1954, Nevins responded with "Kansas and the Stream of American Destiny." Obviously, Nevins thinks the stream of American destiny, its impulse and promise, lies in the tradition of American liberalism, that is, faith in individual freedom and values on which the country was founded. Because Kansas had such a large role in two major American events, in pre–Civil War strife, and then again in the Populist/Agrarian revolt of the 1890s, Nevins wonders how the state contributed to the advance of American liberalism. He finds Kansas wanting: immature, with too shallow an intellectual base, and with too quick an impulse toward letting centralized government control the lives of American cit-

izens. *Still, he has great hope for Kansas, if only we will reassert individual liberties, cultivate what William Allen White calls a "sense of beauty" (see White essay) and make a home here for the nine muses. Nevins appreciates Kansas honesty, integrity, devotion to large causes, humor, courage, adventurousness, idealism. He knows we can fight the good fight, because we have before. He simply wants to see us fight the right battles, on the right side. More than any of the other analysts, Nevins puts Kansas into his own larger, American context.*

*Still, Nevins' address is quick to generalize. And a few of his particulars are unclear (the Wyandotte Constitution prevailed over both the Topeka and Lecompton constitutions, and "Black Jack Pete" is Col. John Pate, at best a minor historical character who skirmished against John Brown in the Battle of Black Jack, June 2, 1856, and who probably does not belong in the same sentence with Brown). Also, Nevins is largely insensitive to much of Kansas culture, unfamiliar, seemingly, with Langston Hughes (*Not Without Laughter, *1930) or with Kenneth Porter, May Williams Ward, William Inge, and the many other accomplished writers and artists (Birger Sandzen and the Prairie Printmakers, for example) of mid-twentieth-century Kansas. Still, when Nevins calls for Kansas to develop a new patriotism, one that includes the muses, the state would do well to answer with all its strengths.*

Patriotism, Herbert Spencer once wrote, with that dislike of nationalism and chauvinism which always marked his thought, is reflex egoism or extended selfishness. As Kansans met to celebrate their centenary, they would have done well to bear in mind that aphorism. It will be profitable, I think, to examine the relations between the hundred-year career of Kansas and the parallel career of the whole republic with special reference to one subject: the contributions of the State to the traditions of American liberalism. But it would be fatuous to do this with a view to flattering the pride of Kansas or indeed of the United States.

In cold fact, liberalism in its classic sense—the maintenance of individual freedom: freedom of thought, of speech, of conscience, of economic and social action within legitimate bounds—has sometimes fared ill within Kansas. It has often been caught in cruel predicaments in the nation as a whole, and in recent times has suffered injury from some terrible and inescapable dilemmas faced by the American people. One dilemma is that of protecting our ancient freedoms while pursuing the inexorable path of consolidation and centralization fixed by economic and social circumstance. All Western nations, however much they cherished individual privileges, have found that the rise of great industrial aggregations to serve thickening populations has required a counterbalancing centralization of political power. This double-headed collectivism naturally places sharp restrictions on individual freedom. From Charles H. Van Hise in *Concentration and Control* to John Dewey in *Liberalism and Social Action*, so-called liberals have defended the growing authority of the state, but the process must nevertheless provoke doubts and regrets. A more recent dilemma is offered by the militarization (a grim but accurate word) of the American people. Caught in what President Eisenhower calls "the age of danger," we must arm heavily for survival; and this discipline means a constant threat of regimentation. We cannot afford to be complacent about the past, present, or future of liberalism either in Kansas or in America.

That Kansas has had a special character and peculiar destiny most of her citizens have always believed. Just what have that character and destiny been, and what have they meant to American liberalism?

One fact is obvious at the outset: that in their respective careers during the past century Kansas and the United States have followed highly divergent roads. The United States has moved steadily along the broad highway of industrialization and urbanization: Kansas has of necessity clung to the narrower lane of agricultural growth. The nation as a whole, stage by stage, has reached a point where 12 or 15 per cent of its population, equipped with modern engineering devices, can produce food for all. This healthful process has released the other 85 per cent for a vast multiplicity of undertakings. It is mainly because of invention and industrialization, which give every American an average of sixty slaves—that is, machine power equivalent to sixty workers toiling day and night—that our standard of living has risen (materially) so high. Our position contrasts sharply with that of India, where 95 per cent of the population strive to produce enough food for the country, and never quite succeed.

As America has become industrialized and urbanized, Kansas has of course taken certain steps in the same direction; her capital investments in industry during the course of World War II were impressive. Essentially, however, she is still a farming State. Thus we have the fundamental circumstance that national destiny and State destiny have in large degree lain crosswise.

Out of this divergence early came a bitter conflict be-

tween the agrarian and the industrial or financial interests,
with much name-calling that we can today grant was exaggerated on both sides. The New York *Nation* in May, 1896,
said tartly: "Kansas now cuts the worst figure of any State
in the Union." What Kansas orators were saying at that
time of Wall Street, Big Business, and Mark Hanna was almost unprintable. The physical scars of the hard years of
the Farmers' Alliance and Populist era were matched by
psychological scars; for Western farmers felt that while the
leaders of the industrial revolution and business concentration were astride a great lurching harrow, and *they* were the
toads beneath, the American majority callously jeered or
reproached the sufferers. "The toad beneath the harrow
knows, exactly where each toothpoint goes"—that was bad
enough; "the butterfly upon the road, preaches content-
ment to that toad"—this was worse.

The conflict, the suffering, and the mutual misunder-
standing gave birth to explosive forces in politics and government. They were the more explosive because Kansas, in
her most discontented period, had a relatively simple class
structure. The State was too young, too homogeneous, and
too poor to have produced any groups like the oligarchic
planter families which played such a part in Virginia's history, or the important merchant elements so prominent in
the record of Massachusetts. The forces were also the more
explosive because the society of Kansas lacked maturity.
Critics of the State constantly reproached it for drabness,
aridity, provincialism, and lack of distinction—and the criticism had much force. A more mature society might have
endured hardships and injustice with greater philosophy,
as Vermonters endure it, or with some such sense of purifi-
cation by tragedy as South Carolinians had after Recon-

struction. But the explosive violence with which Kansas asserted herself as Agrarian Rebel did much to shape and harden the Kansas character, already well individualized.

This great central cable in Kansas history—the stubborn agrarianism of its 80,000 square miles during a century of national industrialization—is the strand on which a thousand events and personal stories can be strung. It gives meaning to the careers of the most prominent leaders of Kansas. Of recent years the force of the Kansas divergence has been lessened. For one reason, modern invention has largely erased the old difference between city and country in America; the automobile, hard roads, telephone, radio, and television make urban and rural life much alike. For another reason, with its government crop supports the farm population has come to share in that Special Privilege it once denounced. Nevertheless, the special character of Kansas, a wheat sheaf and not a sunflower her true emblem, remains.

Both the record and the character must not be oversimplified. Kansas had of course witnessed a great deal of history before the industrial revolution got under full steam in the East after the Civil War. Certain elements in the personality of the State had become fixed by 1870. A long line of writers, from Eli Thayer through John J. Ingalls to Andre Siegfried, have declared that Kansas is the unique Western child of Puritanism. It is that in a special sense. As everyone should know, the original population of Kansas came chiefly not from New England, or from Missouri and the South, but from the middle tier of States stretching from New York and New Jersey westward to Iowa and Illinois. But much as we must disagree with Ingalls in many of his generalizations upon his native State, we can accept his statement that Kansas was largely dominated by the New England mind. Governor Charles Robinson, for example, son of Hardwick, Massachusetts, was a typical Puritan in his abolitionist ideas, his fervent belief in free governmen- tal institutions, his moralistic attitude, his historical in- stinct, and that strong interest in education which did so much for the common schools and the State University of Kansas. He represented a powerful element among the real makers of the common wealth. If Andre Siegfried meant that Kansas was peopled by a Puritan stock, he was wrong; but if he meant that it had a vital Puritan leaven—and of all leavens only the Scottish and Jewish leavens have pos- sessed equal strength—he was completely right.

The Kansas struggle of the 'fifties strengthened this Puri- tanism. It inspired nearly all the Northern poets—Longfel- low, Lowell, Emerson, Holmes, Bryant, and above all, Whittier, who returned to the subject again and again. Overseas it was watched with anxiety by some of the finest European spirits. Byron's widow collected money for the New England ideal of freedom in Kansas, Victor Hugo wrote a pamphlet, and Walter Savage Landor penned verses. Like all such struggles, it was grotesquely misrepre- sented by many participants, North and South. The image and the reality of the Kansas war, so ably disentangled by James C. Malin, are very different. As historians have sepa- rated truth from propaganda, many idols of the antislavery enthusiasts have been overturned.

Yet the fundamental fact remains that on the Kansas plains from 1854 to 1860 was fought a momentous conflict between the idea of freedom and the idea of slavery; that a desperate effort was made by an unprincipled group to present Kansas, in defiance of climate, soil and population,

First Capitol of Kansas, Margaret Whittemore

at least briefly and superficially as the sixteenth slave State; and that the great cause of human advancement won when the Topeka Constitution triumphed over the Lecompton Constitution. Stephen A. Douglas always believed that the Lecompton battle was a salient national turning-point; that if Buchanan had joined him in rejecting that proslavery instrument, the bluster of Southern fire-eaters would have been put to the test before they had fully matured their plot; and that their discomfiture in 1858 would have averted civil war in 1861. However this may be, the moral elements bound up in the struggle along the Kaw and the Missouri strengthened the vein of Puritanism in the Kansas character, just as the violence of the contest nurtured traits of bellicosity and extremism.

A belligerent trait was made plainly evident in the Civil War record of the State. Kansas sent more soldiers to battle than it had voters when the conflict began. It lost more men in proportion to population than any sister State; 61 dead for each 1,000 enlisted. Kansas men fought on practically every field in the Southwest from Wilson's Creek to the Gulf. Provost-Marshal Fry at the end described their proud record. "The same singularly martial discipline," he wrote, "which induced about one-half of the able-bodied men of the State to enter the army without bounty, may be supposed to have increased their exposure to the casualties of battle after they were in the service." In short, Kansans were born fighters. Along that rough plains frontier, they had to be. The affrays of John Brown and Black Jack Pete, even the campaigns of the Civil War, were transient affairs; but droughts, blizzards, chinch-bugs, Hessian flies, grass-hoppers, and tornadoes were abiding enemies. Beginning with the near-famine of 1860, Kansas was always being beset by disaster, and always combating it tooth and nail.

It would be idle to pretend that the civil conflict which lasted from 1854 to 1865, and the harsh struggle with nature which left it doubtful at times whether man could really subdue his environment, did not in many respects lower the level of civilization. If these battles, and this pre-occupation with material trials, toughened and refined some men, they corrupted others. The reminiscences of a sheriff of Sumner County illustrate the grueling ordeal that the Kansas frontier offered.

"I guess," he is quoted as saying, "that the year 1874 was about the worst year that Sumner County ever experienced. First, there was the drought that almost cooked everything, and then came the grasshoppers and cleaned up what little was left. On top of all this trouble came the news that the Indians were about to go on the war path. There was some [Indian] killing, too. Pat Hennessy and some other white men were killed that summer down on the old Chisholm Trail where the town of Hennessy is located." He adds that the horse-thieves were worse than the Indians, and describes a gruesome murder by a gambler and all-round ruffian, who was promptly lynched. T. A. McNeal informs us that Newton was once called the wickedest town in Kansas. But this, he remarks, was a bold statement; "for Kansas in the past has had some towns that in a competitive examination for wickedness would have given Hell a neck-and-neck race." On many men, and on whole societies, the frontier laid a corrupting stamp.

One of the resounding episodes of the political history of the 'seventies was the downfall of Samuel C. Pomeroy—"Seed-Corn Pomeroy"—as he fought for reelection to the national Senate; an event notable partly for the fact that it brought John J. Ingalls, the fiercest master of vitriol since John Randolph of Roanoke, into national affairs, and partly because it illuminated the corruptions that had sprung from early Kansas history. Pomeroy's ruin was accomplished by a courageous rural legislator named York, who laid before the two houses, sitting jointly for the election, $7,000 in bills which Pomeroy had offered him for his vote. The episode shook all Kansas, for Pomeroy had been a powerful man ever since his arrival in the fall of 1854. But what most strikes the present-day student, if he looks up York's speech, is its sweeping indictment of Kansas politics. He speaks of the prevalent corruption, "the deep and damning rascality which has eaten like a plague spot into the fair name of this glorious young State"; and he laments the odium that "has made the name of Kansas and Kansas politics a hissing and a byword throughout the land."

That in the years of Jay Gould, the Credit Mobilier, and the Tweed Ring the name of rural Kansas, Puritan Kansas, could be a hissing all over America, was evidence that the frontier influence had its debits as well as its credits.

But it was not the antislavery contest, nor the Civil War, nor the frontier, which did most to give Kansas its special place in American history and its influence on our liberal tradition. It was, as we have said, the agrarian struggle of the 'seventies, 'eighties, and 'nineties. This etched still deeper the peculiar characteristics of Puritanism, individualism, and belligerency; it confirmed the preoccupation of Kansas with material affairs; and it accentuated the underlying tendencies toward radicalism, a root-and-branch approach to human problems. Kansans had always tended, like their climate, to go to extremes. Now they became more intense than any other equally numerous body of Americans.

Revolutions are not made by utterly impoverished and oppressed societies, by peoples crushed and leaderless; they are made by communities where we find new growth, new needs, new possibilities, and new hopes—frustrated by heavy obstacles. The State was trying all too hard to grow too fast. It had consistently lived on borrowed money, owing the plutocratic East. All the farms, the towns, the counties, had borrowed money. When world prices of crops fell and world prices of gold rose, when credit became as tight a vise as the iron maiden of Nuremberg, the Kansas hope paled. Ominous rumbles heralded a storm rising beyond the flat horizon. At first the distant peals were regarded humorously. More antics by crazy farmers, said the critics, more speeches by wild fanatics, more moonshine platforms which would end in a few more cooperative grain elevators! Then shrewd men suddenly perceived that a true revolution was getting under way. Thomas Benton Murdock interpreted the signs correctly.

"By Godfrey's diamonds, something's happening, young feller," he told a disciple. "Those damn farmers are preparing to tear down the courthouse!"

Caution was thrown aside in the days of Freesoilers against Border Ruffians. "For a generation," wrote Ingalls, while the storm was still rising, "Kansas has been the testing ground for every experiment in morals, politics, and social life. Doubt of all existing institutions has been respectable. Nothing has been venerated or revered merely because it exists or has endured. Prohibition, female suffrage, fiat money, free silver, every incoherent and fantastic dream of social improvement and reform, every economic delusion that has bewildered the foggy brain of fanatics, every political fallacy nurtured by misfortune, poverty, and failure, rejected elsewhere, has here found tolerance and advocacy. The enthusiasm of youth, the conservatism of age, have alike yielded to the contagion, making the history of the State a melodramatic series of cataclysms, in which tragedy and comedy have contended for the mastery, and the convulsions of Nature have been emulated by the catastrophes of society. There has been neither peace, tranquility, nor repose." Such language shows how extremism on one side bred extremism on the other. If the reformers grew passionate, so did the conservatives.

Why did this agrarian revolt, with so much heartfelt conviction behind it, accomplish so little in permanently strengthening the American liberal tradition? For that in the long stretch of American history it did accomplish little there can be no doubt. While it achieved something, we must question whether it took the right path or aimed at the best goals. For two decades the influence of Kansas in the American system was a jutting force: the influence of a homogeneous, old-stock, country-minded people, close to soil, skies, and growing crops, with time to think deliberately and hard, and with the same readiness to debate first principles which the old-stock Eastern yeomen had shown in Revolutionary days. The population in the panic year 1893 was nine-tenths native born, and the rest mainly British and North European. It was overwhelmingly rural. Under the hammer blows of adversity, it was fiercely agrarian in the sense in which John Adams would have used the word. It wanted to break patterns, not solidify them. But did it clearly see what it could best accomplish?

What Kansas Populism did do was to help throw a bridge from Jeffersonian liberalism to the Progressivism of Theodore Roosevelt and Woodrow Wilson. In early days the Western pioneers had believed in the Jeffersonian tenets of rural honesty, independence, and thrift, the restriction of industrialism to a fair balance, and the encouragement of freehold expansion; from government they had desired little but light spending, low taxes, and cheap land. Now they began calling for Federal regulation of trusts, Federal ownership of railroads and telegraphs, a Federal farm credit system, and Federal disaster relief; they looked not to Topeka but Washington. Their program they still called liberalism, but the word had taken on a changed meaning. It is doubtful if they fully realized the implications of their demands. They were anxious to hurry on governmental centralization, but were they willing to give up their old individual liberties in the process? Just how far would this aggrandizement of national authority carry them from Jeffersonian or even Jacksonian ideals?

For some light on the question whether they took the true path we might briefly compare the course of three great farming populations in three parts of the globe who were simultaneously shaken by hardship into fiercely determined action: Denmark, New Zealand, and Kansas. Of these three, Denmark is smaller in area than Kansas, New Zealand larger. From 1875 to 1910 all three expressed much the same temper. Denmark, a farmers' state, now possesses, as a result of measures initiated in this period, an economy planned in the interest of agricultural efficiency and social justice. Its systematic abolition of landlordism, tenancy, and rural debt, its equitable taxation, its social insurance schemes, its statutory encouragement of education and other instruments of culture, and its constant use of the central government as an agency of change, have made it in the eyes of many a model commonwealth. It represents an application of the best yeoman intelligence, on the Socialist plane, to the problems of modern life. Many of the changes, coincidental with the conversion of Denmark to dairying, were achieved in the very period of the intensest Kansas ferment.

Meanwhile, New Zealand, under John Ballance and Richard Seddon, was displaying the same temper and using

the same ideas in reshaping its socio-economic life. Much
more than the Kansas people, the sturdy New Zealanders
had been acquainted with the idea of community planning
from the start; for New Zealand was colonized by the migration of whole communities at a time. To Christchurch,
Dunedin, and other places, settlement first came in a body,
with every calling from minister to blacksmith, every enterprise from store to steamfitter, every instrument of culture,
represented in the arriving shiploads. American visitors to
New Zealand today are astonished at the vigorous social
and cultural fruits of this system of settlement by communities migrating in a mass: the flourishing museums, li-
braries, recreation parks, specialized schools, and even art
galleries in towns like Timaru and Nelson. These Antipo-
deans were ready to use the island government in vigorous
ways. Their insurance schemes, their control of industry
and labor, their equalization of wealth, were even more advanced and rigorous than Denmark's. Like the Danes, the
New Zealanders believed wholeheartedly in cooperation,
and made cooperative agencies work. Particularly after the
overthrow of the Conservatives in 1890, New Zealand rapidly became a half-Socialist, half-cooperative Commonwealth, studied, admired, and denounced around the
globe.

It is plain that the Kansas Populists, for all their heroic
zeal and energy, did not accomplish what the farmers of
New Zealand and Denmark wrought. Of course one reason
is evident. It can be said, with much truth, that if Kansas
had been an independent island-Commonwealth, or an independent peninsula-nation, then William A. Peffer, Jerry
Simpson, Mary Ellen Lease, and their associates might
have done for it what Estrup and Deuntzer did for Den-

mark, and what "King Dick" Seddon did for New Zealand. Instead, Kansas was one of forty States, compelled to adjust herself to Indiana, New York, and California. The New Zealanders, rallying under banners reading "Down with Lombard Street," could shape their own destinies; the Kansas radicals, mustering under the device "Down with Wall Street," had to reconcile themselves to the election of McKinley. "You can't legislate prosperity into existence," said Ingalls, speaking for the East, "any more than you can make rain by legislation." Like the New Zealanders and Danes, the Populists believed that much *could* be done. The whole country believes it today—but in 1890, Kansas had to yield to the national skepticism.

So, at least, defenders of the Populists can assert. William Allen White, ten years after his what's-the-matter-with-Kansas explosion, recalled with contrition the fact that he had derided the Populist candidate for Chief Justice for saying, in effect, that the rights of the user are paramount over the rights of the owner. Since then the world had moved. "The *Gazette* was wrong in those days," he confessed, "and Judge Doster was right. But he was out too early for the season and his views got frostbitten. This is a funny world. About all we can do is to move with it."

Defenders of the Populists can also assert that they did more than this—that they helped it move. They could not remake their society like New Zealand's, but they could set free a leaven which helped alter the texture of national thought. Their destiny ran counter to the destiny of the nation; very well, they would deflect the nation. The Kansas agrarians objected to Manchester Liberalism of the Herbert Spencer type as outworn; they wanted at least the John Stuart Mill type. They fought for the larger governmental activity which, expanding under Theodore Roosevelt and Woodrow Wilson, came into full bloom in New Deal days. They believed that agencies in Washington could be used to protect helpless people from calamities not of their own making, to lessen wrongs and iron down inequalities, and to put science and collective effort in harness for the general betterment. Government might even be used to redistribute some of the wealth and keep it more evenly spread. Everybody believes that nowadays except a few Texas oil men and their like.

The question remains, however, whether Kansans of that era made their proper contributions to the American liberal tradition. One defect of their movement was its glaring lack of a true intellectual basis. Ingalls' phrase about "foggy brains" is unjust; the Kansas leaders, within their limitations, had thought slowly, clearly, and courageously. But the limitations were grievous, for they were relatively uneducated, unread, untraveled, and largely unaware of historic facts or current world trends. Their movement was too much a horny-handed blow at intolerable hardships, too little a hardheaded probing of their social and economic predicament. They contributed a good deal to the spirit of the coming Progressive era, but not much to its stock of ideas. None of their polemics (for they seldom went beyond polemics) is read today; they had no Tom Paine, no Hinton Rowan Helper. Doubtless the embattled Kansas leaders were later respected by the intellectuals so prominent under the Square Deal and the New Freedom—by Jane Addams and Brand Whitlock, Lincoln Steffens and Herbert Croly, Louis Brandeis and Walter Hines Page. But were they much admired? And if not, why?

We may also question whether the agrarian rebels, in trying to throw their bridge from Jeffersonian democracy to Rooseveltian and Wilsonian Progressivism, did not do unwitting damage to some liberal values. Was it in the proper spirit of Kansas to contend so decisively for centralization? It would have been better had they tried to rear Utopia by their own hands on their own 80,000 square miles. The cooperative principle which was invoked so effectively in New Zealand and Denmark could have been made to yield nourishing fruits in our own West. Unquestionably, the obstacles were formidable: the poverty of the farmers in this era, their bondage to Eastern capitalists, the steady blows of rainless years, the fact that wheat-growing is less amenable to cooperative action than dairying, and the before-mentioned position of Kansas as one of a large family of closely connected States. Nevertheless, more could have been done than was attempted. More, too, could have been done to effect self-help through Topeka as an alternative to Federal help through Washington.

Kansas in the days of the stalwart Simpson and Peffer was an inspiring rebel, but it is not so inspiring to the liberal mind as Wisconsin in the days of Robert M. La Follette. La Follette, equally stalwart, was a well-educated thinker. He had an ideal of Wisconsin as a largely self-sufficient commonwealth, where individual liberty would bloom; and the Wisconsin Plan was an effort to use State experts to create State wealth and a true State culture. A series of important laws enacted at Madison made that capital a cynosure of all American eyes. Not Albany, not Springfield, not Topeka, ever equalled it. Under La Follette, the people of Wisconsin were solving some of their problems by their own means. Meanwhile, cooperation flourished—credit unions, land mortgage associations, co-

operative creameries, cheese-factories, and elevators. Was it
impossible for the Kansas leaders of the 'eighties and 'nineties to have adopted some of these measures? Such policies
would have had the virtue of contributing, not to a centralization of governmental power, but to the basic doctrine of
agrarian liberalism, the freedom of the individual.

Perhaps the fundamental lack of Kansas in that period,
and later, was really the quality of maturity. It had the virtues and still more the defects of youth. Its most distinguished sons always thought of it as young, with the impul-
siveness and changeability of early adolescence. They
shared with it these qualities.

William Allen White, for example, outwardly all bland
cherubic placidity, drew from the air of Kansas, like his
friends Fred Funston and Vernon L. Parrington, something
that made him reckless. At the end of his career he recalled
that for sixty years he had needlessly jumped out of bal-
loons and twenty-story windows, and marched through fi-
ery furnaces. Why? He could not tell. He always enjoyed repeating a friend's description of his infantile physiognomy.
"Look at that face," said the friend, "pink and white, fat
and sweet, as featureless and innocent as a baby's bottom!"
But, added the friend, don't let that face fool you. In 1896
White's broadside on the matter with Kansas delighted
Hanna and all stand-patters. And where did he stand just
twenty years later? At the opposite extreme. He was making up his mind that wartime price-fixing should be permanent; that the government should unite the railroads into
one big system, Federally operated; that labor should be
"Federalized" under compulsory arbitration; that income
taxes should run as high as 90 per cent, while death taxes
should take all estates over ten millions; and that compul-

sory military training should transfer every Maine boy to South Carolina, and every California boy to Ohio. Such ideas were less an expression of Socialist views than of the adolescent and changeable spirit of Kansas.

But White was nevertheless an unwearied fighter for more maturity in Kansas; more love for the State, more belief in its self-contained possibilities. He knew that her basic Puritanism, bellicosity, and extremism, were naturally antipathetic to certain finer qualities of life; and only with those qualities could come the adult responsibility and the faith in the power of Kansas to help herself that were lacking in Sockless Jerry Simpson's time. What Kansas most lacks, White used to say, was a sense for beauty. He once told me that few scenes were so entrancing as the rolling miles of ripe Kansas wheat as the grain turns from pale gold to reddish copper; but, he lamented, what Kansas painter had ever caught that beauty on his canvas? "Nothing is more gorgeous in color and form than a Kansas sunset," he writes, "yet it is hidden from us."

The wind in the cottonwoods, the song of the meadow lark and brown thrush, found no echo in the strains of Kansas composers. It was not a Kansan but the Missourian John G. Neihardt who sang of Hugh Glass and the Indian wars on the Kansas plains. Ed Howe, of Atchison, in *The Story of a Country Town*, had given readers a glimpse of the fact that the human spirit could be as tortured in a Western environment, that life could be as harsh, angular, and frustrated, and that a powerful drama could develop as logically from the clash of warped characters, as in Emily Bronte's *Wuthering Heights* or Thomas Hardy's *Jude the Obscure*. Howe's memorable book was published as early as 1883. But neither Howe nor Dorothy Canfield, neither

Meadowlark, Margaret Whittemore

William Allen White nor Paul Wellman, ever widened the vision. That was left for Willa Cather of Nebraska. No writer of fiction has lifted Kansas material to a high creative plane. Until lately, history also had failed to mirror the past in adequate literary terms. All in all, Kansas life of today is as yet deprived of the enrichment by sculpture and music, painting and poesy, which might perpetuate nobilities of the past and nourish dreams of the future.

Until Kansans have a proper sense of what White meant by beauty, their patriotism cannot reach the highest level, nor their liberalism—a faith in individual values—be wholly fortified.

The word "patriotism" in a huge federal republic of 3,000,000 square miles possesses a dual significance. Americans must sometimes think it hard that they have so wide a country to feel patriotic about. Though we do not have to make the choice that Robert E. Lee, torn between America and Virginia, faced in 1861, we sometimes envy the Englishman, with so small a country that he can be affectionately intimate with most of its nooks. Happier still is the Dane, Greek, or Israeli; devotion to 10,000 square miles is naturally more intense than devotion to an area 300 times as large. But the fact is that citizens of our 48 States can feel two kinds of patriotism. Our national patriotism is fundamentally political, based on civil allegiance and the national idea. Our State and local patriotism is fundamentally geographical and sentimental. With the first we associate the idea of power, with the second the idea of place and home. So-called patriotism on any scale can be a poor emotion so long as its main elements are clannishness, acquisitiveness, and pugnacity—the patriotism of the Nazi or the American hundred-percenter. It needs, as Dean

Inge wrote, to be spiritualized and moralized. It must be

hallowed by history, legend, poetry, and art. To this spiritu-
alization State and local patriotism, fed by love of home,
specially lends itself.

Before its people love Kansas with the right fervor, they
will have to make its soil sacred to the nine Muses. Carl
Becker relates that as he once sat in a train traversing the
plains, he listened to some college girls chattering near by.
One maiden, glancing out of the window at the landscape,
delighted him by ejaculating, "Good old Kansas!" With all
respect to Mr. Becker, it is difficult to feel much impressed
by this sort of emotional tribute. If the girl had caught her
breath, exclaiming, "There Stephen Kearny's army set out
for the invasion of Mexico"—if she had quoted a line from
a Kansas poet or orator—if she had referred to the tragic
John Westlock of *The Story of a Country Town*—a subtler
feeling would have been involved.

When Robert Louis Stevenson wandered along the coast
of Fifeshire, he did not stare around him vacantly and exclaim: "Good old Scotland!" He mused to better purpose.
This country of Fife, he recalled, had been transformed by
history, legend, and poetry. Over these commonplace-look-
ing fishing villages brooded the storied past, full of the
quaint, the tragic, and the uplifting:

Dunfermline, in whose royal towers the king may be
still observed (in the ballad) drinking the blood-red
wine; somnolent Inverkeithing, once the quarantine of
Leith . . . ; Burntisland, where, when Paul Jones was off
the coast, the Reverend Mr. Shirra had a table carried
between the tidemarks, and publicly prayed against the
rover at the pitch of his voice and his broad lowland dia-

lect; . . . Kirkcaldy, where witches once prevailed extremely, and sank tall ships and honest mariners in the North Sea; . . . Wemyss with its bat-haunted caves, where the Chevalier Johnstone, on his flight from Culloden, passed a night of superstitious terror; . . . Largo Law, and the smoke of Largo Town mounting about its feet, the town of Alexander Selkirk, better known under the name of Robinson Crusoe.

When the nine muses have a richly decorated home on the Kansas prairies, then the State will be able to boast the warmer kind of patriotism that Scott, Burns and Raeburn gave their little land; then social and intellectual maturity will stamp more of its life; and then the fountainhead of liberalism, a belief in the individual, his gifts, potentialities, and sacred rights, will flow more freely.

That the brighter, broader era will come we need have no doubt. The history of Kansas reveals so many cardinal virtues that we may be sure others will be added to them. Honesty was one of these virtues. The Kansas mind has been a sincere mind. From the days of Jim Lane to the present, the State has produced her share of what may be called demagogues; but she has never had a demagogic agitator of the worst type. Her agrarian radicals might be confused, as Jerry Simpson sometimes seemed, or dryly tedious, as W. A. Peffer often appeared, but they had an abiding quality of integrity. Kansas leaders might frequently be commonplace or naive, but they did not consciously lie, or bring false accusations against the helpless, or appeal to the worse prejudices of their hearers—as one great demagogue in American life today has done. Humor, too, has been a Kansas trait. The State needed it to make its harder years endurable, and blunt its extremist tendencies. One of Jerry Simpson's happiest feats in Congress was to stride down the aisle, pick up the silk hat worn by Dingley of Maine, high priest of protection for the home market, and with a gleeful taunt exhibit its London trademark. Lesser men used humor with frontier ebullience. Once when worse calamities than usual had ravaged western Kansas, her representatives proposed some relief spending financed by a bond issue. Conservatives from eastern Kansas protested. The Constitution did not permit this, they argued. A Westerner at once rose to propose a motion. "Resolved," he vociferated, "that 100,000 copies of the Constitution be printed in pamphlet form for distribution among the destitute people of Western Kansas, to enable them to get through the winter and furnish seed wheat for spring planting."

But of all the cardinal virtues, courage has been the most prominent. Among the forty-eight, Kansas, we repeat, has stood out as a fighting State. Her happiest periods have been her fighting years. The freesoil settlers, the men of the Civil War, and the agrarian reformers never feared the hardest blows. The ideas of Kansans might be bitterly unpopular, from the Topeka Constitution to the Carry Nation ideal of prohibition, and from woman suffrage and State-owned elevators to the Preston B. Plumb plan for national ownership of railways; but their sponsors never faltered in advancing them. They had the backbone to make a boast of the sentence Ingalls used as a reproach: "For a generation Kansas has been a testing-ground for every experiment in morals, politics, and social life."

Even more experiment would have been welcome. Nothing is more important to American progress than variegation among the States. Out of this variegation should naturally flow experimentation in politics, economic arrangements, and social life. State trial of bold innovations is one possible advantage in a Federal nation—too much neglected. It is healthy that Massachusetts should differ in traditions, interests, and ideals from New York, and Kentucky from Michigan. A European might find it hard to distinguish between North and South Carolina; any American knows that oil and water are hardly more diverse. Of all the States, Kansas has been historically one of the most strongly marked. Her stormy history, her steady succession of spectacular figures, her extremist tendencies, give her a unique place in the national scene. From John Brown to Victor Murdock, she managed to make her neighbor Nebraska look pallidly conventional, and Iowa tamely conservative. When Kansas asserted herself, the whole world knew it. May she continue to do so! For the rest of the nation feels disappointed when she relapses toward those genteel norms so well represented by Mr. Landon. Let us hope that after the soft prairie zephyr has blown mildly awhile, the rousing Kansas cyclone will return.

Nothing less than cyclonic forces, properly harnessed, will now serve the country. We live in times far more perilous than John Brown's or Sockless Jerry Simpson's. Our only security is in a fiercely thrusting progress. Externally, we face a continuing threat of the direst gravity—we are truly in what President Eisenhower calls not a temporary crisis, but "an age of danger." Internally, we shall be lost if we do not make rapid progress in science, industry, culture, and social harmony. Kansas may yet do more than in the past to protect our liberal tradition from the dangers inherent in centralization and in militarization. For the ordeal ahead of us we need the adventurousness and devotion to freedom that marked Kansas history in the angry 'fifties; the toughness and courage bred by the later conflicts between an agrarian State and an industrialized nation; and the idealism and vision which run like a golden thread from Charles Robinson to William Allen White.

ONE HOME

William Stafford

William Stafford was born in Hutchinson in 1914, lived in several Kansas towns, attended the University of Kansas, and he went on to a distinguished career as teacher and poet, most recently in Oregon, where he now lives in Lake Oswego. Although he has been named poet laureate of Oregon, his poetry is often set in, and is reflective of, the Kansas he knew in the first half of this century. The title of his first collection of poems, West of Your City *(1960), shows Stafford's stance, his allegiance to the plain but rich landscape of his home. "One Home" celebrates a plainspoken people, secure in their environment and traditions. All of his work has a simple richness, which, like the landscape, yields much to those who examine it closely. Stafford won the National Book Award in 1962 for his* Travelling Through the Dark *and has been the most influential poet of his generation on writers trying to make art from a sense of place.*

Mine was a Midwestern home—you can keep your world.
Plain black hats rode the thoughts that made our code.
We sang hymns in the house; the roof was near God.

The light bulb that hung in the pantry made a wan light,
but we could read by it the names of preserves—
outside, the buffalo grass, and the wind in the night.

A wildcat sprang at Grandpa on the Fourth of July

Road to Bohon, Beatrice S. Levy

when he was cutting plum bushes for fuel,
before Indians pulled the West over the edge of the sky.

To anyone who looked at us we said, "My friend";
liking the cut of a thought, we could say "Hello."
(But plain black hats rode the thoughts that made our
  code.)

The sun was over our town; it was like a blade.
Kicking cottonwood leaves we ran toward storms.
Wherever we looked the land would hold us up.

1960

A LEVEL LAND

William Inge

*William Inge (1913–1973), a native of Independence, is best
known as the playwright who took Broadway by storm with his
Kansas plays of the 1950s:* Come Back, Little Sheba, Picnic,
Bus Stop, *and* The Dark at the Top of the Stairs. *He won
an Oscar for his original filmscript* Splendor in the Grass *in
1961. He lived most of his adult life an expatriate from Kansas, though he returned to the state over and over in his plays,
filmscripts, and novels. After Inge's suicide in 1973, critic
Robert Alain Arthur wrote that the plays contained "the
truth, the absolute truth, about mid-Americans in the mid-
twentieth century."*

*Inge's "A Level Land" also shows how well he knew and
appreciated the Kansas landscape and its effect on the people
who live in it. Inge recounts his own experience with the sky
and what it can bring: drought, flood, tornado, and other violence on the one hand, innocent blue mornings and awesome
sunsets on the other. He notes how a plain landscape creates an
unadorned people, conservative but not extreme, a people
"sweet" because they are dependent on forces larger than themselves, because they know themselves not to be all-powerful. Finally, Inge gives the reader a valuable vocabulary lesson no
Kansan should ignore: the difference between* flat *and* level *is
a difference between whole ways of seeing and thinking.*

The Plains States are the heart of our nation, and that heart beats slow and sure year after year while the cities on the coastlines, crowded, competitively industrial, cosmopolite and more seemingly vulnerable to foreign influences as well as attacks in time of war, manifest our nation's violent anxieties and antagonisms. Nowhere can we find a closer correlation of landscape and character than in the Plains States. The people there are, for the most part, as plain and level and unadorned as the scenery. New fashions, new inventions seldom emanate from this region, and its native artists usually go to some other part of the country to find appreciation and encouragement. In recent years at least, one has seldom heard of riots, strikes or demonstrations in Kansas, Missouri, Nebraska, Iowa, Minnesota and the Dakotas.

Human violence, when it does occur, is all the more frightening because one does not expect it in such a quiet, innocent land. The bloody murdering of a wheat farmer's family in a peaceful Kansas community horrifies us more because of the unlikeliness of the setting than because of the deed itself, which might not seem so grotesque in a populous, strife-torn, industrialized city.

Violence on the plains exists more in nature than in man. A person lives in this mid-country with an inherent consciousness of the sky. One is always aware of the sky in these states, because one sees so much more of it than in the mountainous regions where the horizons are blocked and the heavens are trimmed down like a painting, to fit a smaller frame. And human life on the prairie is more dependent upon and influenced by the sky and its constant maneuverings than in other regions. Men here look at the sky each morning as soon as they get out of bed, to see what kind of a day is indicated. Life and prosperity depend upon that sky, which can destroy a season's crops in a few hours, by hail or blizzards or tornadoes or a relentlessly burning sun that can desiccate the land like an Old Testament curse.

During my growing years in Kansas, I witnessed every extreme of weather and learned that it is as unpredictable in all the Plains States as the pictures that show up on a slot machine. I attended the University of Kansas, at Lawrence, in the early 1930s, when dust storms were periodically enveloping the land. The dust darkened the sun and filled the atmosphere, seeping into houses and stores. There was no way of escaping it. It discolored all the air and made the necessary act of breathing a hazard and a discomfort.

The spring when I graduated from the university, there was a deluge. Between mid-April and early June there were but three days when there was no rain at all. Graduating seniors had to march in the rain to the vast Hoch Auditorium, where we sat in moist attendance in our damp caps and gowns, smelling of wet wool. All the rivers and streams overflowed their banks and the entire eastern half of the state was flooded. Train and bus service was either stopped or rerouted. When the rains finally ceased, the sun came out in full force creating a steamy heat that lasted the summer. The following spring and summer there was a tragic drought. The rivers and streams withered dry, livestock died on the plains with parched throats, and the record-breaking heat (for two weeks the temperatures reached 118 degrees in my own section of Kansas) kept people closed up inside their homes, hanging wet sheets over electric fans to create a semblance of air and refreshment. The entire earth looked as if blasted in a furnace. The Plains States were a partition of hell.

In April of 1938, when I was teaching high school in a small mining town close to my home, I experienced my first tornado. It struck unexpectedly at noon after a still and sunny morning when students and faculty had walked to school with no anticipation whatever of the freakish violence that the elements were preparing for them. About one third of the town, as I remember, was leveled.

But of course there is beautiful weather on the plains. Nowhere in the world is the morning sky such an innocent blue. And nowhere is the sunset more awesome: a burning globe covers the land with a phosphorescent glow before it sinks into the far horizon. When spring comes early, the month of April can be joyous with bright green grass, budding leaves and yellow daffodils. And sometimes the sun is gentle to the summer months, providing days of pleasant warmth and nights that are cool and sweet with the smell of honeysuckle. In October there is a quickening of life when the trees turn orange and yellow and red, and the harvest brings apples, melons and pumpkins to the markets. The new school year is begun by now, and the daytime world is left to the elders, while the young attend classes and cheer at football games. And there is always good hope for a mild winter.

Once a New York friend, a genuine sophisticate who has lived for varying periods of time in most of the world's great cities, told me of a visit to Kansas much as one would describe a chance to sojourn among the Fiji Islanders. "I found the people to be genuinely sweet," he told me. And I believe they are. Perhaps this *sweetness* of character becomes instilled in a group of people who are more depen-

dent upon the elements than are those in other parts of the
country. This sweetness, I believe, is of a spiritual nature.
Men in the prairie states have long had to deal with forces
they cannot always control. They often have to surrender
to these forces and deal with them as best they can. This
surrender to forces greater than one's self cannot but create
a humility in human character that is a part of all religious
faith. Prairie people, most of them descendants of Puritan
New Englanders or of God-fearing Scandinavians or Central Europeans, know and live with the knowledge that
man is not all-powerful. That may explain why people in
the Plains States are (I believe) more solemnly religious
than those in other parts of the nation. There are the fa-
natically religious, too, but they are a small minority. The
general tendency in this level land is to be conservative in
all things, and to be suspicious of all extremists.

But these peaceful states have had their share of dis-
senters. Rebellion is not foreign to them. John Brown and
Carry Nation and Billy the Kid all lived in Kansas. So did
the Communist leader Earl Browder. And the notorious
James brothers came from Missouri. Every town and city in
the Plains States has its share of misfits, people hostile to
the environment, who feel themselves in a broad land that
is full of narrow minds. They seek their destiny in other
parts of the country. Some are criminal; some are creative.
Los Angeles, San Francisco, New York, Chicago, Miami,
Houston, all owe much of their color and culture to these
sometimes gifted misfits from the plains.

When I lived for a while in western Massachusetts
friends liked to tell me about a woman from Minnesota
who had come to the Berkshires for a vacation that she did
not appear to be enjoying. She took no pleasure at all in

Hay Meadow, Arthur W. Hall

the lush, romantic landscape. When asked what she thought of the scenery, she replied, "There isn't any. The mountains get in the way." I appreciated the story and realized that I felt the same way. No mountains can be as beautiful for me as the far horizon, level as a floor, 20 or 30 miles in the distance. The sight fills me with a wonderful feeling of personal freedom, and also with a sense of infinity. Man finds his solitude here and in the still atmosphere cannot help but wonder about the nature of all being.

Not all the land in the Plains States is level. Much of it is gently rolling, and there are a few mountains. But those areas are exceptions in this level land. Level, but not flat. When we speak of anything as *flat* we imply that it holds no content of interest. But we use the word *level* as synonymous with honesty and truth.

Instinctively, I call the land *level*. People who do not appreciate this region call it *flat*. And perhaps one has to be born and raised in the Plains States to see and feel their serene and understated beauty. People from the East are slow to respond to it, if at all. And they deplore its lack of Eastern culture. When I was a boy in Kansas, my family had neighbors who had just moved to our town from Colorado. The mother of this new family never became happy in what she called "this flat country." She became seriously neurotic there, unable ever to feel "at home" or to make friends. She never ceased to long for the mountains that were native to her. Eventually, her husband gave up his job and took her back to Colorado, where they made their home again and have lived happily ever after.

Maybe we find beauty only in what we know. Mountains have never intrigued me. They have none of the mystery of the prairie, where one can always feel close to some eternal truth concerning man and his place in the universe.

[From TIME-LIFE LIBRARY OF AMERICA: The Plains States.
© 1968 Time-Life Books, Inc.]

PORTRAIT OF
A CHANGING KANSAS

Kenneth S. Davis

Kenneth S. Davis, born in 1912, grew up in Manhattan, Kansas, and went to Kansas State University and the University of Wisconsin. He has been a writer all his life: with three novels set in Kansas (In the Forests of the Night, The Years of the Pilgrimage and Morning in Kansas); with a stint as war correspondent attached to General Dwight Eisenhower; with biographies of Eisenhower, Lindbergh, Adlai Stevenson, and Franklin Delano Roosevelt; and with the Kansas volume of the Norton Bicentennial History Series. He now lives in California.

"Portrait of a Changing Kansas" is an excerpt from a speech delivered to the Kansas State Historical Society during the year Davis spent in the state researching the Kansas volume. In it, he explores why Kansas has such a hold on Kansans. His first two sections contain powerful insights into how physical Kansas plays a role in creating the "internalized environment" that makes up the Kansas character. His reflections on Kansans as "sky watchers" who live with and in the wind is personally and poetically echoed in Denise Low's essay, but his insights into how the environment shapes our political contradictions— we are assertive and abnegating, champions of freedom and prescribers of behavior, highly individualistic and conforming— are unique. Although Davis moves on in his essay to a discussion of Kansas as a political entity, the geography lesson re-

mains more potent. For, no matter how ignorant or learned we are about Kansas history, our geography, our topography and our weather remain always with us, shaping us into the Kansans we are, with our "chronic expectation of the unexpected."

To the first issue of the old *Kansas Magazine*, in January, 1872, John J. Ingalls contributed a sketch of Albert D. Richardson, the newspaper correspondent who had "covered" Bleeding Kansas for Boston and Cincinnati papers. Wrote Ingalls: "Kansas exercised the same fascination over him that she does over all who have ever yielded to her spell. There are some women whom to have once loved renders it impossible ever to love again." So with Kansas. The inhabitants of other states, said Ingalls, "can remove and never desire to return. . . . But no genuine Kansan can emigrate. . . . He may go elsewhere, but no other State can ever claim him as a citizen. Once naturalized the allegiance can never be forsworn." (Quoted by Daniel W. Wilder, *The Annals of Kansas*, Topeka, 1875, p. 563.)

The native or longtime citizen of any other state has for it, normally, a certain amount of home feeling—and often this is ambivalent. But he does not normally have any truly vital commitment to the state as a state, does not look upon it as a unique cultural entity, and certainly does not personalize it and then respond to it as a personality attractive or repulsive, or both. My wife, for instance, was born and raised in northern Missouri. She confesses a mild nostalgia for her particular home area when we in our travels pass nearby. But for Missouri itself she has no such regard, pro or con, as I have for Kansas, pro *and* con—no such regard as most born-and-bred Kansans she has met, in or out of the state, have evinced—and she has often remarked with puzzled wonderment upon this peculiar intensity of feeling which Kansans have for Kansas. So have friends of ours, non-Kansans, in the various places where we have lived. "I've never met a Kansan elsewhere whose heart wasn't buried in Kansas," said a friend of mine, a widely travelled executive of a large insurance company in Worcester, Mass., when I tried to explain to him why I was laying aside pressing work to which I have long been committed in order to write this Kansas book. I myself know of no other state, save Texas, whose citizens are as strongly, intensely, personally identified with it as Kansans are with Kansas.

Why is this so? What is this hold which Kansas has over Kansans? How did it develop? What, and *why*, have been the variations in its nature, its quality, over the years?

I

My own several attempts to answer these questions, including the one I've been making this last year, have always begun with a consideration of certain physical facts about the state—facts that have necessarily affected Kansas history and culture and economy.

. . .

On the map, as William Allen White once remarked, "the state . . . looks flat and uninteresting . . ." (William Allen White, "Contemporary Scene," a foreword to *Kansas, A Guide to the Sunflower State*, New York, 1939.) A perfect parallelogram, save for the jagged bite taken out of its northeast corner by the Missouri river, its 82,000 square miles contain both the precise geographical center of the contiguous United States and the geodetic datum of North America. This central continental location, far from the temperature-moderating influence of any large body of water, but directly in the line of air currents flowing north from the tropics, south from the Artic—this makes for swift and wide fluctuations of temperature. It makes for winds more constant and strong than prevail in most states— winds climaxed by the notorious Kansas cyclone, such as whisked Dorothy into the Land of Oz, to the everlasting dismay of the Kansas Chamber of Commerce. It makes for an erratic temporal distribution of rainfall, and for rains considerably more furious than those of, say, New England. Massachusetts is much greener than the Kaw Valley, is criss-crossed with streams of steady flow, and is dotted with lakes, largely because New England's rains come often and gently, most years, and are easily soaked up by a porous forest soil. A Kansas rain, on the other hand, is often so intense that a prairie soil cannot drink it anywhere near as fast as it falls. A high percentage of it runs off, carrying eroded soil into streams whose water volumes greatly expand and contract in relatively short periods of time— streams always remarkably shoal strewn and variable as to depth. This means that flood and drouth may occur within a few weeks of one another during any growing season anywhere in the state.

Here, then, is a country of weather extremes—of blazing heat and bitter cold, of prolonged drouth with its dust storms and torrential rains with their floods—a country of high and temperamental winds which, in their irritability, utter tornadoes with greater frequency than any other state experiences, save two, where the incidence is but slightly greater than in Kansas.

But here, too, overall and paradoxically, is a country possessed of one of the pleasantest and most healthful climates in the nation. Kansas has considerably more nearly perfect days, weather wise, than most states do—has more cloud-free days than any other state of equivalent precipitation—thanks in good part to our long springs and long autumns, which are delightful seasons, almost always.

These weather facts apply to the state as a whole. But within the general weather patterns are significant differences. There are no mountains in Kansas, certainly—no hills more than a few hundred feet high—but one climbs a mountain's height, climbs well over 3,000 feet as a matter of fact, when one crosses the state from east to west. One also moves in steady progression from a generally well-watered country into a country where the annual rainfall though highly variable, is of an average sufficiency for ordinary temperate zone agriculture; thence into a country where rainfall is meager in any average year and becomes more so with each rising 10-mile until, in the state's western extreme, generally semi-arid conditions prevail. And because the surface of any land is largely shaped by water erosion—because the general color of any natural landscape is largely determined by temperature and average annual precipitation, this color being an overall blend of the colors of the dominant vegetation—because this is so there are three quite distinct general kinds of landscape in Kansas, regional landscapes, each coinciding with one of the three areas into which the state may be equally divided, with rough accuracy, in climatic terms.

Of the well-watered *eastern* area, the predominant landforms are those of stream and river flood plains, flat and fertile and varying in width from a mile or so to 15 or 20, bounded by lime-ridge hills bearing upon their crests a various width of rolling prairie. The virgin land in this eastern area bore much timber, far more than did all the rest of Kansas. Indeed, approximately 2,000 square miles of the glaciated northeastern corner is designated on native flora maps as "oak-hickory forest," and streaks and patches of such forest are interspersed on such maps with a "mosaic of prairie and oak-hickory forest" throughout all the area for a hundred miles or more westward from the eastern border. Beyond this, westward, is a 30- to 40-mile band, extending north and south across the width of the state, designated as pure "bluestem prairie." Here are the Flint Hills—limestone hills whose rounded contours are periodically, rhythmically interrupted by stone ridge outcroppings, forming step-terraces. They are treeless, save in their hollows, where a few cottonwoods and scrub oaks rise up in generally meager growth. They present to the traveler through them wide vistas of a surpassing wilderness beauty—a beauty that is much the same now as it was five thousand years ago—for these immense pastures, on which graze a million head of cattle annually, have never been plowed. The bluestem turns a lovely golden brown tinged with blue at summer's end, but during most of the growing season, throughout this eastern landscape, the dominant color note is a vivid blue-green.

Central Kansas has, in its eastern portion, a landscape whose contours are much the same as those to the east but whose dominant colortone, in summer, is a somewhat paler green. The contours flatten out, and the green grows still (it becomes at last a yellow-green) as one moves westward. The limestone undergirding of the eastern section gives way to sandstone, some outcroppings of which have

Coronado Heights near Lindsborg, Margaret Whittemore

been carved by wind erosion into fantastic monumental shapes. The tall bluestem thins out, begins to occur only in clumps here and there, with the rest of the soil carpeted by ground-hugging buffalo grass. Finally there is no bluestem at all, only buffalo grass, and trees are fewer and smaller. The west-warding traveler, entering this country, has climbed onto the Great Plains proper, and he continues to climb onto the immense table land known as the High Plains.

The landscape of these High Plains is predominantly that of the *western* third of Kansas—the portion having the least variety of scenery and the least rain—the portion which early explorers deemed uninhabitable and designated on their maps as the Great American Desert. And indeed there are many today who, coming from afar into this land as it now is, in the fullest state of its development, yet see it as a desert place, an enormous windswept desolation in which there is nothing to charm the eye, nor even any object for the eye to rest upon.

For it remains a largely empty, featureless land. One may travel through it 50 miles in any direction without encountering as many eye-catching things, or anywhere near as many distinctive views (differently composed, differently framed) as one meets in a typical half mile of the New England countryside around my present home. And I have heard not-a-few people wonder aloud how *anyone* can bear to live amid such flatness, such monotony. All the same, I have seen beauty here, as I'm sure have many of you. It is an austere beauty composed, with a severely classical restraint and economy, of the simplest materials. John Noble, the famous sea painter, who grew up on the Kansas plains, once said that the plains taught him to understand the sea—and indeed the likening of this land to the sea, the wind-waved sea, or the sea becalmed, is a simile that naturally and even inevitably occurs. This is a far country, high and pale and abstract. Its landscapes are predominantly skyscapes of which, earth or sky, the slightest detail assumes by its very rarity a large significance. Every variation becomes symbolic. A cloud, a rock, a slight roll of earth on

the horizon rim, a solitary stunted tree standing at the edge
of a shallow ravine—any of these can become the ordering
principle of the whole of one's visible world, with meaningful overtones extending into the world unseen. The overwhelming sense conveyed is of distance *per se*, of empty
space as a kind of ache of possibility—the *really* real. Gaz-
ing out across this land into the heavens, one seems to look
out "beyond time itself" into the Eternal, as Noble once
said (John Noble, *American Magazine*, New York, August
1927, pp. 34ff), and begins to understand why desert places
with immense vistas have been the birthplaces of the greatest religions.

II

Now it is my belief—I suppose my manner of presenting the
physical facts has more than suggested my belief—that the
Kansas landscapes, the Kansas weathers, have had a
marked psychological effect upon the citizenry of this state.
They've had a character-moulding effect; they've contributed to the peculiar emotional hold which Kansas has on
Kansans. They've done so in ways impossible to measure
with any scientific precision—ways which must therefore
be left out of account by any strictly quantifying cliometri-
cian—but which are in perfect accord with the philosophy
of organism (Whitehead's philosophy) to which I myself
have long subscribed. They are implied, these ways, by
Whitehead's doctrine of the integration of perspectives—
his recognition that no entity is ever merely itself but is always *also* its relations with other entities, his conclusion
that connectedness is of the *essence* of all things. No environment is wholly external to the environed. There is in-

terpenetration. When the environed is a living entity, the environment is *actively* internalized, becoming part and parcel of the individual psyche to some indeterminate degree.

And I think that the Kansas weather-and-landscape, as an internalized environment, has made the Kansan in general more aware of elemental forces and of being at their mercy, has bred a somewhat more acute sensitivity to the natural world as both scene and agent in the world drama, than is common among people who live in weathers less prone to extremes and in landscapes having shorter views.

For instance, Kansans are a race of sky-watchers. Of course the sky is everywhere around us in this land of far horizons: it constantly impinges upon the Kansas consciousness. Even where the land is heaped and rolled over lime- or sandstone undergirdings, three fourths or more of any person's level view across it in any direction consists of heavenly space and light with whatever cloud formations drift over it—and even when the sky is closed off and lowering in gray glooms it remains a vast brooding presence. It conveys a sense of high, far, lonely distances. This psychic effect is augmented by the Kansas wind. Even in the eastern part of the state the wind blows more strongly and constantly than it does in most areas. As for western Kansas, it is part of the windiest inland area on the continent. No environmental factor had a greater effect upon the High Plains settlers than the almost ceaseless storm of wind. Pioneer women especially found it hard to bear. A few were driven literally mad by it. The wind's constant physical pressure against their bodies when they went outside rendered tangible terror of immense empty space and harshly accentuated the solitude, the human loneliness of a Plains

farm. The wind's ceaseless thrust of dust through every
tiny crack of door or window, every minuscule chink of
sod-bricked wall, frustrated the most strenuous and unre-
mitting efforts at cleanliness. Above all, the wind's endless
and (for such women) nerve-rasping whispers and whines
and shrieks fed neuroses which grew at last beyond the
bounds of sanity. Such cases were rare, of course. Most of
the people who settled here, women as well as men, grew
accustomed to the wind. Many grew fond of it, feeling the
lack of it, on those seldom days when it failed to blow, as
an unnatural stillness, a disconcerting silence. But this ad-
aptation even where made with no great psychological difficulty, always meant, I think, subtle changes in character,
in personality.

Nor are wind and sky of only psychic import in the making of Kansas character: they also speak directly and em-
phatically to the economy here, in what remains an agricultural area and has historically been almost wholly so.
The Kansas eyes that look into the heavens are *interested*
eyes, economically interested, and their vision is haunted
by historical memories of sky-borne catastrophes. The
drouth and famine of 1860, when thousands of Kansans
depended for their very lives upon relief supplies from the
East. The drouth and wind-riding grasshopper hordes of
1874, when again the survival of thousands depended
upon relief. The blizzards of 1886, in whose blinding snows
and bitter cold perished scores of Kansans on the High
Plains, along with the theretofore burgeoning enterprise of
great cattle barons. The prolonged drouth of the late 1880's
and early 1890's, which cast down the Kansas boomers,
raised up the Kansas Populists, and drove literally hundreds
of thousands out of the state ("In God We Trusted; In Kan-

sas We Busted"). The equally prolonged drouth of the 1930's, with their unprecedented and terrifying dust storms across the whole of the state. All these echo as coloring, tuning memories down the corridors of mind as a Kansan lifts his eyes above the horizon.

Hence the fact that the sky here is not just passively gazed upon as a remote and theretofore pure aesthetic spectacle. It is constantly paid close attention to—is often anxiously and even prayerfully consulted by Kansans who measure against its mighty moods a goodly portion of their personal aspirations, their personal difficulties. In this respect, the state motto, *Ad Astra Per Aspera*, has always seemed to me peculiarly apt. And the sky here teaches what might be called, paradoxically, a chronic expectation of the unexpected, joined to an awe-streaked respect for natural forces whose sudden twists and turns can either overwhelm and destroy, or uplift and enhance, the effortful lives of individual persons and communities. The psychological effect has been, I think, to encourage in Kansans a somewhat greater reverence for eternal verities, a somewhat greater concern for the fundamentals of life and conduct, a somewhat more strict and conscientious regard for moral right and wrong, than is common elsewhere. Also environmentally encouraged has been a fluctuating blend of seeming contradictions—a blend of self-assertion and self-abnegation, of rugged individualism and a passion for conformity, of strong insistence that the human person is free and an equally strong insistence that he act in certain prescribed ways—that even his private tastes and personal conduct are fit subjects of legislative action.

This peculiar blend has been present here since pioneer days.

Self-reliance, self-confidence were prerequisite to any pioneering move onto the wild Western frontier. No man could make this move who did not believe that his personal strengths and skills were sufficient to overcome whatever obstacles and hazards he might encounter. But this faith can also be defined in terms of the possible obstacles, the hazards: the pioneer had to believe that these would not be so great as to crush him. His plunge into the unknown involved a species of fatalism. Optimistic fatalism. He took a chance as he moved onto the frontier. He tested his luck, in the optimistic belief that his luck was good. Which is to say his *self*-reliance was mingled with its precise opposite, namely, a reliance upon the *nonself*—upon outer forces which were admittedly more powerful than those he possessed but which, he trusted, would prosper rather than destroy him. To this extent, every pioneer was possessed with a gambler's psychology—for of the essence of the experience of any chance taking, any gambling game, is this sense of placing oneself at the mercy of outer force; of making as one places his bet, an existential leap. Even with the pure gambler, however, chance taking is seldom if ever an absolutely *pure* existential leap. Almost always the gambler attempts to propitiate the fates, or Lady Luck, by means of certain gestures, magic rituals, certain signs or acts. He does things he believes to be lucky—avoids things he believes to be unlucky. He has superstitions. He *is* superstitious.

But in the early Kansas settler's case, the representative early settler, this gambling fatalism was by no means the whole of the story. It was intimately linked if not substantially merged with something much more deeply felt and highly organized, something much more respectable intellectually, namely, the prayerful reverence and ethical concerns of religious faith. Specifically, predominantly, it was a Protestant Christian faith of the Puritan variety whereby, as a matter of fact, the typical Kansan was rendered *hostile* to gambling, to all forms of gambling games, on moral grounds. Gambling games yielded pleasures having sensual overtones, and it was the Puritan's conviction that spiritual prosperity must be paid for by sensual deprivation.

Part and parcel of this religiosity has been, over the years, the Kansan's genuine concern for the welfare of his fellow man, spiritual as well as physical. Sometimes this has led the Kansan to conceive himself to be literally his brother's keeper, with a moral obligation to coerce his neighbor as well as himself into quite narrowly defined paths of righteousness. And I think this last has been encouraged by the manifestation of God's wrath which the Kansan has seen in dust-darkened, blizzard-blanched, storm-blasted skies; he has felt he had reason to fear the Lord's chastisement of the whole community if individual members of it succumbed, even in the privacy of their own homes, to the devil's temptations of alcohol and extra-marital sex. This, however, is but the least attractive manifestation of the Kansan's religious concern. There have been and are, attractive manifestations as well—a genuine respect for the rights and feelings of other people, a scrupulous regard for the laws upon which a civilized society depends, a real human warmth and kindness and generosity in times of trouble, a generally prevailing human decency that strikes with a particular force of contrast anyone coming here from Eastern urban centers.

BREATHING KANSAS

Artful Goodtimes

*Art Goodtimes first became acquainted with Kansas during
what William Least Heat-Moon calls a "Great Kansas Passage." Stopping to breathe Kansas during harvest work one
summer, Goodtimes realized that one had to walk the ground
to understand this place (or any other). "Breathing Kansas" is
his poetic response. Goodtimes is one of a long line of poetic
travelers to conjure with Kansas: Walt Whitman; Vachel Lind-
say, the Vagabond Poet; Harry Kemp, the Tramp Poet; even
Allen Ginsberg, the great Beat poet who celebrated Kansas in
"Wichita Vortex Sutra."*

Art Goodtimes works as a journalist for the Telluride (Colorado) Times-Journal *and is poetry editor of* Earth First, *an
environmental magazine. He won a 1989 fellowship in creative
writing from the Colorado Arts Council.*

For the Hitz family of Montezuma

*"Chants going forth from the centre of Kansas, and thence
equidistant shooting in pulses of fire ceaseless to vivify all. . . .*
                                                    —Walt Whitman

        Work Work Work Work Work Work Work Work
is the ethic that drives the tractors
crustbusting across the buffalo wallows.
                        Breathe it in.

Joy on Kaw Valley Loam, E. Hubert Deines

It's Kansas tumbling big skies between cottonwoods. The
   high plains where all is horizon. Mud track farm roads
   that run on forever.
In Garden City, Hutchinson, Emporia pollyannas in pig-
   tails
still dreaming up tornadoes & along US #50
monuments to wagon ruts still cut in the clay of the Santa
   Fe Trail.
All the Kansa
          people of the South Wind
marched off to Oklahoma, intermarried
leaving only stories & the mystery of names:

Topeka, Chicopee, Oskaloosa.
                    Breathe it in.

The centerfold primerib wheat heart of America.
Whitewashed steeples where the minister stands
shaking hands loose from pockets.
Windmills. Feedlots. Grain elevators.
Blue out to grass & wind blowing strong.
Out here in the plowed fields
night's a morse code of farm lights mimicking stars.
Daytime thunder crackles. Clouds plume & vanish
                    Breathe it in.

It fills the lungs with distance. Legs stretch out
with the Kaw, the Smoky Hill, the Arkansas. Rivers drying
    up
go underground as the pumps feed the pipes that circle like
    vultures.
Fears root in with the sinking water table. Dwindling fuel.
Dust storm eyes irrigate themselves.
But in a good year one's whole field of vision
gone bushel-green & sprouting. Sunflowers & futurities.
Snow on the milo & heads on the stalks. Threat of hail &
    harvest rush.
                    Breathe it in.

            Breathe in this land
this rolling pasture
this underneath us steady earth heaving like the Mother
    sea

prairie swells rippling with grain.
Breathe it in.

Know this home for what it is: scarred belly of the Turtle.
The wide-angle open-eye buffalo heart of the continent.
Let it breathe within you.
Be inspired
by what breathes beneath your feet.

STRAIGHT ROADS

Peg Wherry

Peg Wherry was born in Des Moines, Iowa, received her B.A. at the University of Northern Iowa in Cedar Falls, and moved to Kansas in 1972. She's been in Kansas ever since, first as a graduate student at Kansas State University, Manhattan, where she received her M.A. in English in 1974, then at Seward County Community College, Liberal, where she taught English and worked in continuing education. More recently she has worked in continuing education at Kansas State University and pursued graduate study in English at the University of Kansas, Lawrence, thus combining her interest in literature and continuing education.

"Straight Roads" is a lesson in the almost continual education afforded the immigrant to southwestern Kansas, where Wherry spent five years. She tries to pin down what fascinates her about this place Kansas novelist Paul I. Wellman once called "an extension of hell." Like many travelers, Wherry begins learning as soon as she stops thinking about destination, about the immediate, and learns to really see. Her perceptions—of landscape, freedom, open space, the straight roads, and the lack of distractions—all create a powerful sense of what in Kansas can either intimidate or intoxicate: a sense that one is alone, without distraction from "man and his conventions." What better help, what better joy, she concludes, than in the "headlong rush to your destination?"

Wherry's writing style reflects the same headlong rush, and

*in her personal approach to understanding the Kansas environ-
ment she connects with other essayists (Davis and Low) who
know they must come, first and alone, to terms with a state
they have chosen, and loved, and then chosen to love.*

I pop open a beer, shove a tape into the player and head on
down U.S. 287 south from Lamar, Colorado. I've spent Labor Day weekend in the mountains, and it's time to get
back to Liberal, Kansas, to work. The window is down,
since it's cool and I'm on paved road, and the wind whips
my hair and the sleeve of a T-shirt with Thoreau's wild
stare ironed on the front. Joni Mitchell's *Hejira* drifts on in
tempo with my own, as it has so many times before, and I
can forget enough about the road to soak in the landscape.

Now, down out of the mountains, this trip is like so
many others out here: wide horizons, wind, space, music,
and the rushing of the car and the fenceposts and the lines
on the pavement. I'm in an immense region running from
Mexico to Canada between U.S. highway 81 and the
Rocky Mountains. Few people live here. It's an unspectacu-
lar landscape by conventional post-Romantic standards,
but it has its own compelling attractions.

The country coarsens for a while south of Lamar.
Abrupt drainages that fill with water only a few days each
year criss-cross the landscape. Boulders are strewn about,
and the rough edges of rock show through thin, pale soil.
Bedraggled evergreens that I like to take for juniper are pre-
scient of mountain conifers. The rest of southeastern Colorado, though, is flat and open as far as the eye can see, the
western horizon a pregnant swell promising mountains.
Soon a landmark slides into view: Two Buttes—two

smooth, almost unnatural cones of rock, protruding as if by mistake from the wide flatness. The one to the south is slightly higher; otherwise, a connoisseur of mammaries would agree: Two Beauts. I keep my eye on them. As soon as they pass from view to the north, I watch for my corner. I have to turn east on a Colorado state highway to get to Johnson, Kansas, and thence Liberal.

I could keep heading south on 287 and go to Campo and then east to Liberal. I would like to go through Springfield and the rest of Baca County—I like Baca County, because few others, besides the natives, do. But that route means gravel roads, and I don't want to run the air conditioner or eat the dust or, for that matter, slow down. In this country, you can really drive. I maintain an unpatriotic 65 on U.S. 287, and the semi I'm tailing moves over from time to time to let me pass. But I know my limits—and my car's—and keep my distance. The Labor Day traffic is noticeable, but not troublesome, and vanishes entirely once I'm off 287. In the next 60 miles or so into Johnson, I see only two oncoming vehicles, and none on my side of the road. There are exactly two curves. The hen pheasants on the roadsides are plentiful—closer to home, I accidentally hit one, and the feathers flutter in the grillwork for days.

As I approach Johnson, I plan my route the rest of the way. I finally determine to go south from Johnson a ways, then east to Richfield, south to Rolla, and on to Second Street Road and east to Liberal. These country roads are so gratifyingly dependable. You have in mind a general direction—say, in this case southeast—and you just keep turning south and east until you end up some place you recognize. The roads are absolutely arrow straight except where a river bed or large wash may be more conveniently crossed at an angle or where the survey lines didn't come out even at state or county lines. Take Second Street Road, for example. It gets off to a tricky start in Liberal, since Second Street itself ends in the Beech Aircraft parking lot. But if you jog around the perimeter of what used to be Liberal Army Airbase, the road straightens out—a full 45 miles without a curve, until just outside of Elkhart.

On straight roads, I remember Mike Felder, an honest good-hearted guy from WaKeeney, who tended bar in the club where I worked back in Manhattan (Kansas, of course). Mike said once he thought he'd like Iowa—he'd seen a map, and it looked like Iowa had a lot of straight roads. Mike really trusted straight roads, and now I understand. Ed, whom I have helped with our college Outreach program, driving all over seven counties, said the same thing. He didn't like northern Minnesota. He felt claustrophobic—all those trees, and the roads wound around all over the place, and you couldn't see the towns until you were right there. I always liked northern Minnesota, but I'm beginning to like these straight roads, too. It's not just the lack of surprises and the relaxed vigilance. There is a certain liberation in being able to move directly toward your destination in a headlong rush.

On Second Street Road between Elkhart and Liberal there are four or five weatherbeaten stop signs, which are usually ignored, even by women with small children sliding off their laps. There's a gesture at compliance, and of course you must look both ways as you slow down. If the corner is in wheat stubble or grazing land, cutting back to 50 while checking out the horizon is good enough. If it's milo or corn, you might have to slow down a little more, and if there's someone following, you probably ought to drop clear down to 30. If I'm in the college van with "Home of the Saints" written on the sides, I stop, but I feel a little silly and excessively formal.

There's a lot of familiarity along these roads and many conventions of traffic movements are dispensed with. Very few lines are painted on the roads, for example, and sometimes the grass grows out over the pavement, blurring the edge of the artificial surface. There are (praise heaven) no billboards—in fact, there are few signs of any kind. Occasionally at a corner is a large arrangement of narrow boards, all weathered and indecipherable, giving directions to neighborhood homesteads. And there are county line signs—county lines are important—but usually no state line markers except the requisite notices about weight limits and stopping for school buses when the lights are flashing. If you don't know where you are in this country, a sign saying "Welcome to Kansas"—or Oklahoma or Texas or Colorado—is not going to help.

Not only is it assumed that you know where you are and where you're going out here, it is assumed you know everyone else on the road. On the county roads, the state highways, even the lesser traveled U.S. highways like 156 between Garden City and Larned, all the drivers wave. Not a fruity, television-commercial flapping of the hand back and forth, though. Perhaps it's not really a wave at all. More of a salute—one or two fingers of the top hand on the steering wheel are lifted during a split-second of eye contact as the vehicles pass. Hell—there ain't no strangers out here. Anybody on Second Street Road is one of us.

I remember the summer of 1976, trying to lead-foot a U-Haul truck out here with all my worldly possessions. It rained around Great Bend and Larned, I remember, but it soon cleared. It was cool, and there was a rainbow in the east that I could see by turning my head just slightly. Straight ahead was a technicolor sunset, all orange and gold and huge. Taking it all in, I figured I was making a good move, and later that night, I knew it. The U-Haul ran out of gas just north of Liberal. The first vehicle to come along stopped, and the two farm hands said if I was still there when they came back from "setting water" up by Sublette, they'd bring me some gas. I was, and they did. A few years later, I skidded on January ice and smashed up my car on a bridge. Once again, the first passers-by offered to call the sheriff from Sublette, and, in the meantime, I listened to the coyotes howl and bewept my outcast state. I loved it. Anybody near the Cimarron River on a winter's night is one of us.

Some farmers hereabouts have started growing sunflowers as a cash crop. Sunflowers are supposed to be phototropic, though I've never seen them move myself. I remember only a whole field of them on the road to Hugoton, standing rank on rank, heads hanging heavy, leaves going limp, facing east like a dejected army. And I thought to myself what an appropriate symbol the sunflower is for Kansas, where the population seeks ordered uniformity and dutifully faces east.

I never thought I would see the day when I agreed with Spiro Agnew, but he was at least partly right in identifying an eastern media establishment. Yes. Yes, it's there—the amusement or condescension or rare wonder with which the commentators send their occasional messages from the heartland. Oh yes—the heartland. A nice, hokey name for a nice, hokey place inhabited by nice, hokey people (or *folks*, as Charles Kuralt would say). I resent the amusement lurking beneath serious dissections of Iowa political processes in January and I resent superficial attempts to convey the energy and significance of the Kansas wheat harvest in July—attempts that fail to capture its almost monomaniacal intensity while missing the pointed irony of an effort that is frequently a losing battle for the farmer.

And I don't even belong yet to this strong, quiet, eastward-bowing society. I may be a native midwesterner who spent the best years of my youth in rural Warren County, Iowa, but I've only lived "out here" six years, long enough to know it's not long enough. Heckman, our resident artist, puts on a mock western voice and snarls, "We don't like strangers." But that's not it, really. I'm not a complete stranger to rural America. This country is just a little different from where I grew up, and so are its people. I like the people, despite their shortcomings as perceived by the eastern media. And even though I'm not fully acclimated, I've been here long enough to resent the judgments of others upon us.

Take, for instance, a recent book about Baca County, Colorado. The authors never say their book is about Baca County—they give no place names and doctor their photographs to protect their secret. Maybe that's how they got Baca County to cooperate. But anyone familiar with this country knows it's Baca County under inspection, and anyone who reads a map can figure out where "the southeasternmost county in Colorado" is. The authors are sociologists and I suppose their book met with approval from their colleagues, as the study of a culture different from their own. Oh, the man was a native of Denver, but he got his masters in sociology in Michigan; the woman was an easterner, coming to Walsh, Colorado, by way of Sarah

Lawrence and Princeton. Not surprisingly, these two find Walsh (pop. 900) rather constricting. They make a pass at appreciating the sweep of the landscape and the toughness of a native population who have managed to survive in such unpromising circumstances. But they find life in the small towns confining, limiting, debilitatingly conventional. They are oppressed by the lack of imagination, by the insularity. They talk to a high school teacher (also an outsider) who is depressed when he looks through a recent yearbook and counts the kids who are married and living in town, married and living in town.

I recited this to Heckman, a high plains native who stopped out long enough to get an MFA, and he jumped in to make the point. Suppose you took some folks from Walsh to Sarah Lawrence and asked them what they thought. Or go through a high school yearbook from any city in the country, large or small, and get depressed at the number of graduates who are married and living in town, married and living in town. And where would contemporary artists be without a belief in the narrowness, the shallowness, the debilitating conventionality of modern American life in the cities and suburbs? Let the sociologists study the inner city, the suburbs—the dark places, the winding twisted places—and leave our clean high plains alone.

Living out here, we have reason to be a little "different." This is a country where even to look at the landscape is to accept a dare. The land is rough inhospitable buffalo grass and yucca and sagebrush, miles and miles of it, and a huge scary sky—but if you want to make the effort, it can be exhilarating to try to feel significant in such an enormous place. Ever since I took the dare one splendid May morning, discovering the Cimarron River valley en route to Liberal for

a job interview, I have been somewhat perplexed by tourists
who whine about what a boring state Kansas is. Maybe
they just don't look closely enough. Maybe they have no
sporting blood.

True, this is dust bowl country. Even irrigation, hailed
here as the greatest technological advance in agriculture
since the plow, doesn't help much. The wind blows fiercely
hot in summer—our severe season—and if the usual 15 to
18 inches of moisture doesn't come in winter, by spring the
land is at the mercy of the winds. The first spring I was
here, the dirt blew as it hadn't for nearly twenty years.
Even my students had seen nothing like it before. The air
was choking thick, everything seen through a tan cloud,
and the world looked like an old daguerreotype. You
couldn't see from building to building and roads west of
here were closed. I was teaching Eliot that day: "I will show
you fear in a handful of dust." My students failed to catch
the potency of the allusion—they were too busy watching
the roof of the Pizza Hut disappear and reappear through
swirling clouds in the college parking lot.

The dirty 'thirties changed this country. Towns faded
away. Old homesteads fell apart. Some stayed, some survived, and relics abound. Sometimes on Saturdays in the
fall Heckman and I drive around the country taking photographs and drinking beer. We search for and find the old
things—wagons, buckets, barns, stone fence posts, scare-
crows, water tanks—and then Heckman paints them all
winter. Sometimes he calls me late at night while he's
painting something particularly tedious like the wood grain
in a bucket, and we talk about these old things and why
they haunt us. We finally decide that it is not that these
things are useless. It is their very utility that makes them

sad. At one time, the things were essential solutions to problems of everyday living. The wooden buckets, the pumps, the early machines have been abandoned to give people more time. But nonsense—people always have the same amount of time—we just always want more ways to spend it on ourselves. Heckman and I look for the old things and solemnly appreciate the heroic struggle they represent—and then try to joke our way out of sententiousness.

Poet John Garmon, born and raised in the Texas Panhandle, writes that he kept looking for something that stuck up, that broke the horizon line. Those small things, whether old or new, attract more of our attention since all the rest of our world is so undifferentiated. I took a photograph out near Johnson: huge swirling summer gray clouds above an expanse of wheat stubble. The sky was great, but the picture was missing something, some little thing in the foreground to focus the attention—an old tire, a bucket, something. "A fence post would have done it," Heckman said. And he should know. He paints this country all the time. He knows how much he has to cheat. "See?" he tells a watercolor class during an outdoor session. "You have to exaggerate a little. Make this rise just a little higher, make those hills just a little bluer. If you paint it as it is, no one will believe you." The high plains are tough for landscape painters. Heckman uses tube after tube of raw sienna. Driving to Wichita one October afternoon, he looked out the window and said defensively, "See? That's the color Kansas is." Or consider lines. The horizon may become boring, but at least people out here understand perspective. The vanishing point is real. The road goes straight ahead, getting ever narrower until it drops off over the edge.

When we go on college canoe trips in the Ozarks, I am almost glad to get off the river after four days. I get tired of being able to see only a little way ahead and behind and of feeling hemmed in by the woods along the bank. It occurs to me that river people must develop a sort of tunnel vision. But perhaps those accustomed to a river would feel as frightened by all of our space as I do by all of their twists and turns and impenetrable banks. I understand now what I once heard about the expanse of prairie landscape sometimes driving pioneer women mad. But it works the other way, too. My sister felt claustrophobic living in the mountains of western Maryland. The sun went down so suddenly, and she could never tell what the weather was going to do. Out here, you can see the fronts move in and out by looking at the sky. You can watch for miles across the plains as scattered showers fall on one section while others lie still in a weird sunlight. You can see the fine gray veil of rain that swoops down in a graceful curve, sometimes torn off before reaching the ground.

Larry McMurtry, another Texan, quotes a description of this country "where the sky determines so much." Yes. The sky is better than television sometimes. I remember one incredible sunset that I watched all the way from Coldwater one winter evening. A thin strip along the horizon was clear, but most of the rest of the western sky was a wide, upward slanting sheet of clouds that turned from gray to pink to yellow to gold and back through pink to gray again. There were four of us in the car—not terribly well acquainted—and the conversation trailed off as the sky changed. We were all watching it, but no one wanted to be the first goop to say so. Finally Ed ventured an understatement: "Nice sunset, isn't it?" Oh yes.

Kansas Harvest, Mary Huntoon

There are other things to see out here where the sky is the feature attraction. Moonrise, for example, is sometimes shocking, when the moon is full or nearly so. It sprawls obesely over the horizon, not like a moon at all. You look twice sometimes before you recognize a moon—it is just a few wisps of cloud until you realize the wisps are contained in a perfect circle. The moon sits on the horizon for a while, corpulent, diffuse, almost incoherent, then pulls itself together as it rises like a person with a hangover. Sometimes this happens in tones of pink that bleach to white as the sun rolls further away. Sometimes it's orange. At times the full moon in this open landscape can be almost bright enough to read by. One night, huddled in my sleeping bag against the mosquitoes of Baca County, I was awakened by moonrise. It was astonishing and confusing until I recognized the moon and not the sun.

Man-made objects, too, have a distracting clarity. By day, the grain elevators of a town creep up over the horizon and pull your eye their way for six or eight or even ten miles. At night, lights of farms and feed-yards and towns dot the landscape and define the horizon, without ever really getting in the way. The blinking red stoplight at the junction of U.S. highways 56 and 83 in Sublette—the only stop sign in 65 miles—can be seen from over six miles to the north. I always stop at this one, because I've been looking at it for so long it would be rude not to.

All this will change, of course. It is changing now. Malodorous feed-yards and packing plants taint what we brag of as pure air. All the fine particles produced by a growing human population and their cars and their new coal-fired power plant at Garden City will soon obscure the Sublette stop light and the stars. Each spring more quarter sections of sage and yucca submit to the automated ministrations of irrigation sprinklers to become fat-cat carpets of alfalfa or healthy but barren corn fields. And people here think it's progress, like the folks back home who seem not to mind that the cuddly hills of Warren County are being turned into golf courses and mobile home parks. (I suppose this is romantic poppycock. The same growth that brings detestable coal-fired generators and other excuses for spiritual malaise also makes possible such luxuries as public radio. So we beat on against the current.)

I love this country. I love the rush of driving along

county roads hell-bent for Ulysses or Satanta or wherever. The landscape pushes in and pushes in and I finally burst upon the thought "I love—" and then I'm stumped, trying to think of a direct object. Just what is it that I love? This country, of course, but there's more to it.

One night on the way to Hugoton it hits me. Here's what it is, I tell myself—the thrill of an apparent lack of restraint. There's nobody around to watch you run the stop sign or to catch you speeding—or at least you *feel* as if there's nobody around, which is what really matters. No distractions by man and his conventions. A freedom from restraint and a corollary intensity of one's own pursuits. The headlong rush to your destination. True, there *are* stop signs and houses and irrigation pumps and grain elevators and even county sheriffs, but they can all be easily ignored in favor of the sky and your own individual momentum.

Another night, I'm on Second Street Road, driving back from Elkhart and watching the moon pull itself together. Queen and huntress, chaste and fair, I think, indulging in an allusion. I turn the dial to our local public radio station and behold!—well-bred graduate student voices reading William Carlos Williams. "Only the poem/Only the *made* poem/can redeem us." The reading is followed by piano music. And of course, of course, it's Beethoven's "Moonlight" Sonata, played for my own personal enjoyment as the moon gathers intensity. This, I think, this is the way to have it: listening to splendid music as I rush headlong across Kansas, running stop signs under a rising moon.

THE GREAT
KANSAS PASSAGE

William Least Heat-Moon

*William Least Heat-Moon's "The Great Kansas Passage"
comes as a welcome antidote to the image of Kansas as a "fly-
over state" or a place to drive through at night, when all landscape is the same. Least Heat-Moon, in describing the elaborate preparations of travellers readying for their Kansas
passage, shows how they want Kansas to be difficult, even
dangerous: a hard trip links them to the pioneer experience of
over one hundred years ago. Of course, most could cross Kansas, as he says, with an open window and a Grapette. Remind-
ing us that even Coronado (our first tourist) was disappointed
because he expected something different from Kansas (he
wanted Quivira), Least Heat-Moon advises us first to seek a
place and people concerned with the immediate, with real
things. Second, he sees Kansas at the center of the continent as
an image of balance, a still point where tumult settles down.
This is not the usual image of a Kansas on the cutting edge of
reform and political movements (Becker, White, etc.). Instead,
it shows a transition into seeing Kansas as a place more reflective of the past than the future, a place to get in touch with
what was and is, rather than what will be.*

*William Least Heat-Moon, born in 1939, is a self-confessed
Missourian. In his widely acclaimed travel narrative, Blue
Highways, he went in search of what is usually off the main*

*road: places and people who live out of the mainstream, jet-
stream, interstate highway stream of contemporary America.
His view of Kansas reflects that interest. He is currently at
work on another book, this one with Kansas as its locale.*

The memory of my first witnessing the Great Kansas Passage has, like an old sock, a hole or two in it now, but the shape and texture are still recognizable. That first occurrence happened in late July of 1947, a warm evening of cicadas chirring out their sharp-edged presence in the vaulted branchings of the elms along the street. Forty years ago the war had not been over long enough for people to cease speaking of it, especially on evenings like that one when the steady and pleasing rhythms of the suburban streets seemed to remind men of what they had relinquished for almost half the decade. When the husbands and fathers and uncles stood in the glow of their cigarettes near the corner streetlamp while they talked and watched the living room lights come on up and down the block like signals from one station to another, I think they were taking the compass of what they believed—or hoped—they'd fought for. The children sat curbside and waited for the dusk to yield to a good cover of dark before beginning a game of kick-the-can. On such an evening, I saw the Great Kansas Passage begin in a next-door driveway.

The neighbors stood in the laughter and completions of their goodbyes to friends from Scranton, Pennsylvania; the visitors were reciting their route, trying to foresee its peril, readying themselves to press on into the last leg of their journey, that final segment from Kansas City, Missouri, to Colorado Springs. After arriving stiff in the knees and weary in the eyes the night before, they had rested most of the day. Now, from the street corner, the children and men watched the easterners prepare their Pontiac Chieftain for the westward traversing. At the passenger-side window hung a new-fangled tubular device with a concave opening on the front end that made the machine look like a small jet engine. But this contraption did not produce thrust or heat; rather, in the days before refrigerant air conditioners, it supposedly created cool air. The thing worked by drawing in wind over wet filters and throwing a damp breeze into the car. We had heard that, on the desert, the coolers helped, but, in the humid summers of the middle latitudes, the machine turned the car interior into a place suitable for growing ferns and mosses. That evening, the Pennsylvanian poured water into the cooler, then moved to the front of the car where he hung twin canvas waterbags with red stenciling on them from the heavy chrome bumper (those were the days, of course when items could be hung not only from bumpers but from door handles, grilles, trunk latches, hood ornaments; the traveler never wanted for a protuberance to tie down a loose line or wet swimsuit). Every now and then, the waterbags oozed a drip, thereby cooling themselves on the same principle as the evaporative window unit. The easterner had already taken pains to attach a chrome sunvisor above the windshield. Clearly, he thought himself ready for Kansas. We watched the last of the loading: two Thermos bottles and a metal cooler (the kind that left a square of rust over whatever it sat on) painted in the red Scotch plaid of the Stuart clan.

The Pennsylvanians had waited out the sun and now, with the last of the dusk, they were ready to head out, to drive—appropriately—through the old Oregon and Santa

Fe trails jumping-off place called Westport, to pass over the Missouri line, and then, already sagging in the damp air, the waterbags oozing, the speedometer locked down (as best one could on two-lane roads) at seventy or eighty, the darkness protecting them, their cache of sandwiches secured in the back seat, and, finally prepared, to *cross Kansas*.

"Are you set, Marie?" the man asked his wife. He spoke in the tone Magellan may have used when he was ready to hoist sail in Seville to begin his great circumnavigation. She nodded grimly, her mouth pinched closed. They climbed in. She knew they were about to leave the elm-lined streets of Kansas City. She knew that between them and the cool and forested altitudes of Colorado lay that great historic rectangle of discomfiture, that mythic expanse of national character-testing, that place that had done in pioneers by the thousands, that treeless, flattened, featureless, godforsaken, overheated, numbing 82,264 square miles called Kansas. After all, Marie had seen the westerns and had heard the stories. She worked her Dentyne with a D-Day ferocity. She knew the time had come at last for her to *cross Kansas*.

They disappeared into the last light as they headed toward U.S. highway 40: Topeka, Junction City, Salina, Hays, WaKeeny, Oakley, and, if they were lucky, the blessed western stateline. There would also be Tonganoxie, Terra Cotta, Black Wolf, Yocement, Hog Back, and Voda, but they knew that—at least for outsiders—Kansas was a place only to pass through, a place to keep moving in and thereby lessen the chances of a mechanical or a spiritual breakdown. Whatever Zeandale, Moonlight, Hyacinth, Smolan, Munjor, or Milberger held for them, they would never discover. In Kansas you didn't monkey around; you just drove and drove, and you drove fast, and you drove at night. The Pennsylvanians didn't mind driving hard or being driven hard by fear and preconceptions. After all, everybody crossed Kansas that way because everybody "knew" that the least that could happen there was to get trapped in monumental dullness. And wasn't it a tidy and sanity-saving fact of topography that if crossers left Kansas City at sundown and held to seventy-some miles an hour, they could reach the Rocky Mountains just in time to turn around and look out the back window to see the sun begin its own zillionth half-hour-long crossing of Kansas? The travelers would learn that the only thing, other than numbness, to temper the joy and relief at having crossed was the knowledge that home now lay on the other side of the state; the return trip loomed like an appointment with the dentist.

We people of the Missouri border grew accustomed to these passages and the elaborate mental and mechanical preparations they brought forth. I do not remember any of us ever telling easterners—or Californians for that matter—that we ourselves crossed Kansas in the summer with only the windows rolled down and a stop now and then for a cold bottle of Grapette. They would never have believed that we made the journey armed only with common sense based on experience; rather they'd have thought us self-mortifiers like those who follow the Stations of the Cross on their hands and knees, where the goal is not travel but penance.

We stateliners also grew used to the reports eastern travelers gave after their Kansas crossings, accounts that would describe a grim land tediously flat. None of us ever challenged the notion of coastal people that Kansas has all the depth and fascination of a highway centerline. Because we were Missourians, we had no obligation to defend our neighbor (historically, the two states have gotten along like the Hatfields and the McCoys, Popeye and Bluto); but even in our silence before purblind Bostonians and New Yorkers or San Franciscans, we understood that they knew nothing about Kansas except the driving time. (Here I should qualify such a generalization: in fact, once, a Virginian said to me, "When I go through Kansas next month, will I be near Dorothy's house?" I asked who Dorothy was. "The one in the tornado. The one with the Wizard." That passed for eastern knowledge. But recently I learned that Dorothy's house *now* exists in more than just the imagination of L. Frank Baum's readers. Somebody has actually built one.)

Today, nearly four decades after my first witnessing the annual summer event, I see those Kansas passages differently. The preparations of the Pennsylvanians, although needless, weren't as purely ludicrous as we had thought. The piling of equipment and gumption and will were part of the very purpose of their vacations, although I don't think they realized it. What they wanted almost as much as the Colorado mountains was that dread Kansas planogram. They subconsciously wished for a genuine American pioneer experience, a trial that would approximate the grand one that shaped the country, one that has come almost to define the nation. What the couple from Scranton desired was westering. Within their easy comforts and switch-on atmosphere, they wanted a sharing of the danger and mystery of crossing a portion of what was once known as the Great American Desert. Those people wanted to be

in history, and they hoped for immersion in a historical reality, they longed to touch something elemental, if for no
other reason than to give counterpoint to the picture-post-
card world of the Front Range of the Colorado Rockies.
Entrepreneur-developers would, by the next decade, recognize that urge to build "historic" theme parks that kill the
history they feed off. Instead of snickering at the vacationers, we should have perceived the honesty in their attempts
to turn four hundred and more miles of Kansas concrete
into the Santa Fe Trail. Perhaps our own blindness has
helped bring about the rise of Six Flags over Polyvinyl His-
toryland.

But an easterner's nervous anticipations and preparations were useless. Crossing Kansas in 1947 just wasn't that
difficult any longer. Yes, one might encounter a surly pump
attendant, a sour waitress, or a deputy sheriff looking for
his quota; but with a fast car, new tires, and a good bladder,
one need never even set a foot down in Kansas. And, unless the crossing were at night, it truly was hard even to
imagine the region as a desert beset with angry and horsed
red men; to do so required the specter of darkness when
anything could have waited beyond the narrow spread of
the Seal-Beams. Then one could ignore the fields of wheat
and oats and corn, the courthouse towers and Christian
steeples, the chickenhouses and porchswings in the abundant land, and in their stead the outstater could envision—
from behind the Saf-T-Glas—dried up waterholes, Com-
manches, bison skulls, and the yellow gleam of prairie-wolf
eyes.

It was those night crossings that eventually turned Kansas from a region curious and well formed into something
more assumed than seen; in the perception of the nation,

Kansas became a preconception. Night passages put the lie on the face of that historic land of hills, trees, prairies, streams, weird stone outcroppings, and hundreds of villages promising (and usually delivering) good fried chicken and milkshakes. The mythic Kansas of this century became a distortion even more removed from reality than the Kansas of nineteenth-century myths. When vacationers returned to our street at sunrise two weeks after their first crossing, they had become "authorities" on the country between the great, eastern bend of the Missouri River and the Rockies. They would say: "Nothing out there" (at better than a mile a minute, a night rider of blacktop truly can approximate an encounter with nothingness); "it's so flat" (a dark highway has no hills); "so boring" (where are Burma-Shave signs when we really need them?). A Kansas acquaintance of mine, Fred Miller, alleges that some natives actually encouraged these nocturnal passages in order to keep the state out of sight of a coastal America that has long been packing people in tighter and tighter, but he saw no cause for worry since it has always taken a bold person to give up the sure confines of a city for the unnerving openness of Kansas. The kindest remark about the region I ever heard from a New Yorker was, "There's a lot of air out there." Indeed, it is a fact of history that the massiveness of air, sky, and horizon disturbed even the first settlers who quickly found themselves longing for the protective enclosures of forest.

A few years ago, Fred picked up two college boys from East Orange, New Jersey, who were thumbing their way to San Francisco. Between Topeka and Paxico the conversation became spirited, so much so that one of the hitchhikers made a predictable comment about Kansas topography. Fred, who rarely sneers or hurries a rebuttal, said, "Do you have a couple of hours to waste on Kansas?" He turned off the four-lane highway and headed transverse to the usual route of outstaters; he showed them Kansas longitudinally instead of latitudinally, and he presented them the country in the clean light of an early autumn morning. He has yet to divulge that route to me, but when the tour was almost over, one of the thumbers said, echoing Dorothy's comment when she and her canine arrive on the other side of the rainbow, "Toto, I don't think we're in Kansas anymore." But Fred and his riders *were* and had been the whole time. When the boys got out, they thanked Fred—as penitents, he claims—and he answered that the real way to thank him was never to mention the truth of the land they had just seen and to keep spreading the word that Kansas was the billiard table of the gods.

Fred now says that he's sorry he let his chauvinism get the better of his judgment, and he wishes he'd kept a few of those cats in the bag. His response, historically viewed, is quite that of the ancient Quiviran Indians who did nothing so well as to convince Coronado that the seven golden cities lay on beyond the horizon, and, by so doing, to earn themselves another couple hundred years' reprieve from the horrific onslaught of culture from the Old World. Fred, by the way, denies in the face of evidence of some substance that he once wrote the Kansas legislature to suggest a new state motto: Keep scowling and tell them Colorado is that-a-way.

Not every Kansan, I assume, agrees with the Quiviran–Fred Miller concept of improving the territory. Even though I confess a sympathy with the view, as a writer I must try to speak the truth of a place. So what is the truth of Kansas? Let me begin with what everyone "knows": Kansas is flat, flat, flat. No, no, no. While one might describe with accuracy the horizon in the Kansas west of the hundredth meridian as smooth and unbroken, regular and apparently level, in fact, Kansas is marvelously tilted; that's how the Colorado Rockies can make their slow way, granule by eroded granule, eastward to end up in the Gulf of Mexico. A billiard table? If you were to set a cue ball sized to the state on the western border, on its four-hundred mile roll eastward it would drop about three thousand feet (more than three Empire State buildings) and crash into Missouri (an idea appealing to some Kansans). The ball would, of course, depending on its path, have to get over the Blue Hills, the Red Hills, the Chippewa Hills, the Smoky Hills, the Flint Hills, the Chautauqua Hills, and around any number of stony and upright natural obstructions like Castle Rock, the Chalk Pyramids, Mushroom Rocks, and Rock City (maybe bumper pool would be a more accurate metaphor), not to mention rivers and the eastern woodlands. Nevertheless, travelers who think they have seen all of Kansas in one glance from 38,000 feet, and "know for a fact" that it is flat, may need to disabuse themselves by pedaling a bicycle from Westport, Missouri, to Kanorado: let them on their way tell their legs, "It's flat, it's flat."

What else is the truth about Kansas? It is, as the license plates once said, MIDWAY U.S.A. If you cut out a cardboard map of the forty-eight contiguous states and place it on a tack, the point of balance will be near Smith Center. Knowing, then, that Kansas is the geographical heart of America, it would seem reasonable to assume that the state is a place of middle distance, a sort of topographical com-

promise: neither too far west, east, north, or south. It
would appear indeed a place of balance, the spot at the
center that holds comparatively steady in the revolutions
of the "outer" nation. California may be drifting north,
New York may be sinking into the Atlantic, but Kansas
holds staunch. It has come to seem a place of equipoise, a
still point, a region where movements end rather than begin, a land where the tumult settles down to the mere business of getting on with real things—basic things like bread
and beef. (My Kansan grandfather used to say, "Kansas
means eat as in meat and wheat.") But, apparently, all of
this suggests to an outstater that Kansas is only something,
at best, to be thankful for. It's never something to seek out.

If Kansas appears a wholesome, middle ground without
the fascination of extremes, does it then have to follow that
middleness and goodness equal dullness? Certainly in the
early days of Anglo Kansas—the mid-nineteenth century—
as the territory was being cut away from the Rockies and
shaped into a state, things were hardly in a condition of
equipoise, and, most unquestionably, they were not dull.
No state came into the union more violently (hence the ep-
ithet Bloody Kansas or, more touchingly, Bleeding Kansas).
By then the European descendants, as elsewhere around
the world, had successfully bilked the native peoples out of
their land and had settled into cutting up each other over
real-estate promotion schemes and the slavery question.
Kansas did not begin as—nor is it now except in outstate
preconceptions—a land of placidity and dullness. Just consider some names: William Quantrill, John Brown, Bat
Masterson, the Dalton gang, Wyatt Earp, Wild Bill
Hickok, the Bloody Benders, the Clutter family of *In Cold
Blood*. Even names of a less sanguine history give off an

Cowboy Statue, Dodge City, Margaret Whittemore

aura of uproar: Carry Nation, *Brown v. Topeka Board of Education.* The truth is that Kansas history is a tumbling of guns, torches, hatchets, and knives. It is a tale that has always cut to the bone, and that sharpened edge is not reviled by the people: the traveler today can find a monument or museum to all those names but one (and surely the Clutter Museum of Atrocity is right now in some developer's plans).

So what is the truth of Kansas? This is what: Kansas is a complexity of moving points, a land of tilts and shifts, a region full of lives and ideas going this way and that and not infrequently colliding. It is the heartland of America, indeed, but not simply in the way popularly understood; it also beats at our center because, like the whole nation, it moves in turbulence, in fitfulness, and, somehow between times, in beauty. Its motto could be the nation's: *Ad Astra per Aspera,* to the stars through difficulties. Kansas, as well as any other state in the Union and far better than most, embodies the archetypal issues of this country, the movements—both splendid and evil—that formed Americans into something so distinct from the Eastern Hemisphere ancestors: Indian dispossession, the westering movement, slavery, cowboys, bison hunts, women's rights. It is a spacious land of wheat, beef, and oil (American translation: hamburgers and automobiles). On another scale of things American, it is the birthplace of the dial telephone, Mentholatum ("the Little Nurse for Little Ills"), the first white woman to explore the Pacific (Osa Johnson), and the first black woman to win an Academy Award (Hattie McDaniel). It was the first state to ratify the Fifteenth Amendment (black voting rights); what is perhaps the most significant social movement of the sixties, school desegregation, formally started in Topeka. If Kansas is without the athletic idleness of ski slopes or surf, it holds the energy of our national force, import, and interest.

Therefore, I submit this notion: to see Kansas aright is to find much that belongs at the heart of the United States; like the nation, it is a place to be seen in the light of its days and in the shadows of its history. It is not a country to race across enfolded in the obscurities of speed and darkness only to arrive at the foot of the mountains at dawn as though one had slept through it all.

NOT IN KANSAS ANYMORE

Robert Day

Robert Day was raised in Merriam, Kansas, attended the University of Kansas and the University of Arkansas, and has taught at Fort Hays State University. He is now in the English Department at Washington College in Chestertown, Maryland. He returns to Kansas for hunting season, for summers, for academic sabbaticals, and for inspiration for his essays, stories, and novels. He is best known for The Last Cattle Drive, *a novel that takes 250 cattle from Hays to Kansas City in 1976. In it he depicts contemporary life in the state, both east and west. His novellas are* In My Stead *and* The Four-Wheel Drive Quartet. *His most recent book is* Speaking French in Kansas, *a collection of fiction from Cottonwood Press of Lawrence.*

Robert Day not only makes fiction out of Kansas history and culture, particularly Western Kansas, but often makes Kansas into a fictional place. As he writes in "Not in Kansas Anymore": "Kansas is real, sort of." Although Day's portrait shows a Kansas as eccentric in its ruralness as Washington, D.C., is in its urbanness, his point is one he often sounds in his work: Western Kansas may be a place of eccentric individuality, but it is more open, honest, and grounded—closer to what is real—than its opposites—Eastern Kansas, or, in this case, "Our Nation's Capital." For Kansans, then, Day's warning is real: "Keep the bone in your head from getting bent."

*"Not in Kansas Anymore" is satire, and humor comes first
here. But between the lines, Day goes right back to the question asked in the book the essay's title derives from, The Wizard of Oz (1900): Which extreme is more rare, more important, Kansas or Oz? As the scarecrow tells Dorothy after she
explains her affection for "dry, gray" Kansas: "If your heads
were stuffed with straw, like mine, you would probably all live
in the beautiful places. . . . It is fortunate for Kansas that you
have brains." And remember, Oz's Emerald City is a place
very much like Day's "Our Nation's Capital." So why look for
a Yellow Brick Road or somewhere over the rainbow? We have
Kansas, and home, a place increasingly celebrated by Kansas
literary writers for its eccentricities, its differences from mainstream urban culture, and for its steady and constant values
that keep all of us from bending the bones in our heads.*

The man on Pennsylvania Avenue is reading *The Washington Post* to the FBI building: It doesn't seem to be listening.
The man in question is bearded and angry, although the
anger in his voice has taken on that cynical clip you no
doubt acquire if you read *The Washington Post* to the FBI
building over a very long time and it begins to dawn on
you it is a building that doesn't listen.

"As the name indicates," goes the angry bearded man to
the FBI building, thumping *The Post* with his index finger
and reading as though reciting verse, "photo radar / will be
a device / to take pictures / of the license plates / and the
drivers of vehicles / exceeding posted speed limits / by
more than a significant set amount."

Behind him, a mammoth crane is backing up, a *now-hear-
this-or-die* beeper blaring away; its huge bucket swings in

the air. Two women hurry down the sidewalk, one talking of Jesse Helms, polyester suits and photographs of naked black men she has just seen in a nearby museum. Across the street, a platinum limousine, roughly the size of Southern California and with a device that resembles a miniature Stealth bomber mounted on its roof, is negotiating the most sweeping U-turn in the history of western civilization. Traffic backs up to all our embassies in all the corners of the earth.

"Photo radar," the man continues, "would reduce the instances / in which officers must approach cars." Here he pauses and looks over the edge of *The Post* with the meaningful gaze of a Berkeley philosophy major circa 1968. Still no response from the FBI building. The platinum limousine has completed its half-the-globe semicircle and double-parked beside the crane, which, although standing still, continues to bleat away, as if going backward is the *idée fixe* of its existence. Overhead, three low-flying helicopters rattle toward the Potomac in a self-important formation. No one gets in or out of the platinum limousine; it idles like a casket. Down the sidewalk, two men, both carrying what appear to be water-buffalo brief cases from State Department assignments in Goa, walk by in conversation about the "arrogant stiffness" of a local Italian wine store: "One should never recommend an '80 Biondi-Santi Brunello even if one's father does know the owner." But of course. Tell it to the black windows of the platinum limousine, tell it to the philosophy major reading *The Washington Post* to the FBI building. Tell it to Jesse Helms. Dan Quayle. Tell it to me. It will remind me I'm not in Kansas anymore.

Kansas? Do I make a cheap joke at the expense of Toto, Bob Dole, Marshal Dillon and all the other faux naif knockabouts who claim to inhabit that fictional black-and-white square of wheat and populism somewhere west of Falls Church? No joke at all: It's my territory as well. Kansas is real, sort of. In fact I've just come back from a year out there only to descend into the equally "sort of real" world of Washington, D.C., and its environs.

It's a potent drink, these mixed realities: dry martinis at Nathan's, whisky and tomato beer at the Palomino Tavern. But drink up: This story is about you—especially if you are no more from Pennsylvania Avenue and the pastures that surround it than am I. Together we will find a small truth in the text that here abounds, to wit: You *can* go home again; it's leaving more than once that gets tricky.

"Is that true, Bobby?"

"It is," I say. I am talking to my neighbor Banger. Banger lives in the back of a '60's Pontiac station wagon that he has buried nose first in the side of a low hill on his hardscrabble ranch. The buffalo grass has restitched itself over the trench Banger had to dig; if there is rain in the spring, small prairie flowers bloom on the ground above the hood. You don't know Banger and his car are there unless you come at them from the east and can see the back end open in the hill, the tailgate down.

We are in western Kansas. It is late summer. Already it has been 106 in the sun. We don't measure heat in the shade in western Kansas because we don't have much shade, which is why Banger has buried his station wagon: The earth is Shade City. Besides, a big suburban station wagon has ranch house space: Banger sleeps in the middle seat, reads in the front, and watches the world go by out of the back-facing rear seat. A three-room "deal" as he calls it.

In winter, Banger moves himself to his one-man A-frame, complete with a wood burner, two windows and not much more. It's down in a draw so the November through April wind doesn't eat him alive. In some final version of Banger's dream estate, he wants to have his entire deal underground: The earth, he says, is a "thermal battery. Cool in summer. Warm in winter." In his mind he sees one day a stovepipe sticking up through the sod puffing cottonwood smoke out into the blue white of Januarys. But the best things in life take time. That's okay by Banger. Time's free.

"So," Banger says just to get it straight, "when they tear down a building in Our Nation's Capital, they leave up the wall that's on the street." Banger is asking about "facadism"—that distinctly urban practice, begun a few years back, whereby Washington and other cities started saving the fronts of their historic buildings while tearing down everything else.

"That's right," I say. In Kansas, Washington, D.C., is always called "Our Nation's Capital," a phrase we learned in high school civics classes and continue to use in the hope that language alone will keep the Circle City of Government true.

I am being questioned about life in Washington because the men out here—Banger among them—know I've spent 20 years in and around Our Nation's Capital, and they are curious, in their direct way, about what it is like. It is also true I have just spent the previous year among them, living with my wife in a small cabin we keep on the high plains as an amulet against the fury of civilization. Why Banger is asking about facadism, how he has come to know about it at all, or why it interests him, he does not say. The month before—when Banger and I helped a friend move cattle—he wanted to know about the "hill" of Capitol Hill: its size, sidewalks, trees and what you could see from there once you climbed to the top. Now, Banger considers his new line of questioning by looking at his beer and then, for a moment, out at the yellow buffalo grass that is his 2,000 acre lawn.

"And the reason they leave the front that's on the street side when they tear down the building," asks Banger in a flat voice that keeps irony at bay, "is because they made themselves a law that tells them to do that."

"That's right," I say. "It's to keep the past alive. History."

We are silent for a moment while Banger thinks about this. Heat on the prairie has no noise. The nearest road is miles away. The station wagon has a lean-to canvas porch out the back of it. Banger stirs slightly on the tailgate. I am sitting in a stock saddle draped on a square bale. Just beyond us is a foot-long section of pipeline iron that has been converted into a cooking grill. Off in the shelter belt—a circle of trees that protects home places against the wind— you can see a shovel with a roll of toilet paper slid down over its broken handle. If you walked up the hill to the west above Banger's deal, you might catch the distant ka-thud of some doctor-lawyer oil well, but probably not. Overhead, contrails etch the sky for a while, then fray like old rope. Nothing that just passes through this country is remembered. Coming and going in the Russian olives and dusty cedars of the shelter belt are turtledoves. If you were down there, you could hear them cooing.

"Now," says Banger, "suppose you wanted to have a vacant lot behind the building you tear down in Our Nation's Capital where you could keep a horse on a cinder block."

"Yes," I say.

"Would you still have to leave the front of your building standing?"

"You would," I say.

"History," he says.

"Yes," I say.

"And the windows," he says. "Would they still be in the building that's history?"

"They would," I say. "In the front."

"So if you don't want anyone to look at your horse on the cinder block, you can pull the shades in the windows?"

"You can," I say.

"And that wouldn't be against the law about history and the front of the building?" he says.

"No," I say. "Only you wouldn't have any way to pull the shades on the top floors."

"No stairs," says Banger.

"They'd be gone," I say.

"I see," Banger says. He grins. The trick out here is not to let on exactly what's so funny. "Pull the shades and light the light, I'll be home late tonight." He doesn't sing it, he just says it.

Banger and I have known each other for a very long time. He is worried that living on the East Coast might have rearranged the bone in my head. That's what we say out on the high plains when someone has lost sight of the singular madness that is necessary to get from January blizzards to the May tornadoes, and from there to the August branding irons—all on beans and rice, a little whisky, and no doubt some crooked cigarettes: Don't let the bone in your head get bent. Bent head bones can lead to rounded edges, polished boots, fashionable women and trucks with stereos in them. It is thought you can disappear into such a world and never be seen again as yourself.

Banger eases off the tailgate and climbs forward into the bowels of his station wagon. He settles in behind the steering wheel and looks at the dirt packed up against the windshield. The earth's weight has cracked the glass like a star, but it does not sag. Banger's dash is a shelf for paperbacks. He punches in a cigarette lighter that still works; he loves the modernity of it. From over the visor he takes his rolling papers and, looking into the mirror, says:

"You going back?"

"I am," I say. "I've come to tell you that."

"I know you have," he says.

"Going to leave the end of the week," I say.

"Will you give me a hand before you go?" he says.

"Bull calves?" I say.

"The ones we didn't cut last fall," he says. He has rolled his smoke and burns the end of it with the car lighter. Bits of paper curl in flame and fall away as ash. I can see him in the mirror, grinning through the smoke.

"I'll give you the calf-fries to take along when you go," he says. "Prairie oysters once a week keep the bone in your head from getting bent. It's medically proven."

"I believe it is," I say.

It has been a long, deadly drive across the country from Kansas to D.C. Interstates are the straight white teeth of the pretty people who have the conversation of cheerleaders or television actors. Coming down 270 off the Pennsyl-

Summer Afternoon, John Steuart Curry

vania Turnpike, my wife and I are trying to recall how the Beltway works:

"Some of the government gets out at 4," she says. "Or is it 3?" Neither of us remembers, and, although it is a matter of timing to avoid "the crunch," the question is moot because neither of us has a watch and our truck's clock is stuck at 8:32, which is when we dropped the front end over a washout in Banger's pasture the morning before we left. We are south of Frederick and coming in; we are getting lost in some way we don't fully understand.

Our sense is that the plethora of German cars streaming

around us have corporate jet cockpits complete with various crystal rectangles that flash Time of Arrival, Miles Per Gallon, Average Trip Speed, as well as other useful and urgent data. We have heard there are television maps on board these days. We imagine for a moment that by the lightest touch on the tiniest slate gray button in our truck we can project ourselves onto a deep green cathode ray tube carbide with red and yellow corridors. A chart of our whereabouts. We see ourselves, a throbbing white dot, coming back from someplace not on the map.

In the left lane, a Mercedes Man who has ebbed and flowed beside us for three or four miles is in earnest conversation on a telephone. He is shaking his head "no" and pounding the steering wheel with his free hand: A promotion has been denied; a deal sprung loose; a senator backed into a corner. Command is hell, lonely. But that's what you get a hundred-plus K for. Ahead, he spots an opening and surges beyond us onto the bright white lanes just opened. Nothing we see looks all that familiar.

"I hear," says Banger as he sits in his front seat smoking, but looking straight ahead now and not in the mirror, "that Bob Dole has his own parking place."

"He does," I say.

"And more than one office."

"Probably," I say.

"Which means more than one parking place."

"Probably," I say. We stop and think awhile. Then:

"Has anyone told Bob Dole," says Banger, "about the woman in Russell who talks to St. Peter in her basement?" Russell, Kan., is Bob Dole's hometown.

"I don't think so," I say.

"St. Peter tells her Bob Dole's going to be the next and last president of the United States. Maybe he should know."

"I think you're right," I say.

"Sometimes," Banger says, "I sit up here and imagine I'm driving through the earth of America." He puts both hands on the wheel.

"Where do you go?" I say.

"I have some Blood Indians I know near Browning," he says.

"Why don't you drive back to see me?"

"To Our Nation's Capital?" He looks up into the mirror.

"Yes," I say.

"Where would I park?" he says.

Ten miles out from the Beltway and descending into a thick fog of brown construction dust and grimy traffic, we begin to spin the radio dial: Bach fugues; Mayor Barry and cocaine; Handel's Water Music; someone has shot his wife and children to death, then shot himself but lives, comatose; a new book on lobbyists in Washington has been published; Saint-Saens through Stravinsky; a full report on world events at 6. And everywhere on every airwave, some traffic artery that we thought was blocked the year we left is blocked again—or still. It is, we learn, Three-Oh-Seven in the afternoon. And counting.

Coming into it finally, we wonder if we'll remember which ramps and loops and lanes navigate us east around the Beltway toward College Park, instead of south toward Cabin John: both places where we have never been—now that we think of it—and where we have no friends. Indeed, it occurs to us that most signs off the Beltway point toward strange lands, and although we know roughly where we are in our mind's eye, we know as well that the memory of our mind's eye is no match for the sprawling reality of the urban planner. New slabs of concrete create different horizons: In a circle of a city, who checks the sun to see which way you are going?

Ahead, in the traffic of one government or another, it turns out we make the correct banks and turns and we find ourselves stalled in the direction we wanted to go. More dial spinning. More Bach. Some Mozart. A story about the buffalo commons: In the next decades the high plains will become "depopulated." Buffalo is low-cholesterol meat. It grills nicely in Potomac over low coals. It eats its own grass and is natural to its area. No hormones. No steroids. Great herds will be visible out both sides of the aircraft on the morning flights to the West Coast. The larger towns of the plains will be fenced in. History circles back to life. We clutch and brake. Ahead are hills of cars. More Mozart. The familiar hostility of talk shows.

"Is it true," says Banger, "what they say about the buffalo?" We are standing by his working shed; the dust from the steers has settled. A bucket of prairie oysters is hanging from a harness hook where the barn cats can't get them. It is noon. Maybe.

"What about the buffalo?" I say.

"That the government's going to bring them back," he says.

"I don't know that," I say. "What do you mean?"

"They think we're going belly up out here because everybody's leaving."

"Everybody *is* leaving," I say. "What's that got to do with buffalo?"

"Just 'cause you're leaving," says Banger, "doesn't mean I'm leaving." He points at his chest. "I'm here." Behind him some prairie chickens rise as a covey and slap and glide deep into the pastures. Sometimes you don't know what to say, and it feels good.

"Do you know about the buffalo?" I say to the man reading *The Washington Post* to the FBI building. He will not catch my eye. "They're coming back to Kansas." There is a ricochet of light in the street: Someone has gotten in or out of the platinum limousine, but no one has seen it happen.

"Do you know how you drive in Montana in the earth of America?" I go on. Nothing. "Have you heard about St. Peter and Bob Dole?" Still nothing. Maybe he thinks he is on "The Oprah Winfrey Show" and, being male, it is best to keep quiet. "Pull the shades and light the light?" I say. The platinum limousine rocks slightly and moves off, commanding traffic. I realize I am worried about the bone in my head getting bent. I wonder if the man I'm talking to has taken the cure.

"Have you ever seen history in a horse tied to a cinder block behind a building that has only its front?" I say, this time more to the FBI building than anyone else. "The earth is a thermal battery," I go on. "Photo radar has not recorded Banger's deal. We all come from Kansas."

The man who reads *The Washington Post* to the FBI building hands me his paper and walks down the sidewalk. I'd take it with me back home, but on Pennsylvania Avenue in Our Nation's Capital, who can see a rainbow, much less find a Yellow Brick Road?

TOUCHING THE SKY

Denise Low

Denise Low grew up in Emporia and has degrees from the University of Kansas and Wichita State University. As teacher (currently at Haskell Indian Junior College), editor (formerly with Cottonwood Press, Lawrence), book reviewer (Kansas City Star), and poet, she has shown a particular sensitivity to and interest in Kansas and the Midwest, especially the natural life of the region. Titles of her recent collections of poetry reflect this interest: Quilting *(1984),* Spring Geese *(1984),* Learning the Language of Rivers *(1987), and* Starwater *(1988).*

Low's essay not only teaches a great deal about the natural history of Kansas, but shows the more personal history of a Kansan becoming first aware of, then fully appreciative of an undervalued landscape so many natives and outsiders consider flat, dull, uninteresting, or unimportant. As such, Low's essay is the record of what many Kansans, particularly our artists and writers, have had to slowly learn about the state as they have stayed in the region to create their art. Low's attention to place, its subtle beauty and nearly hidden past, might help alleviate the fears of fellow Emporian William Allen White, who, in 1922, wondered when Kansans might begin to penetrate the mysteries of the prairies and the wide skies at night. And Low's essay sounds similar notes to Robert Day's, though without the exaggeration and flamboyance that are his trademark. As such, she comes directly out of the tradition of poet William Stafford.

I. FLINT HILLS JOURNEY

Trees refuse to follow from Topeka.
The car radio loses contact
and mumbles fuzz to itself.

The highway bisects a moonscape
and you are alone.

If you see a diesel truck
it lumbers like a beast
lost from another age
like you.

Two sounds rise from the gullies
and repetitious hills out there—

   in summer
   wind and waves of cicada drone;

   in winter
   only yelps of wind.

The movie *The Wizard of Oz* stereotypes the prairie lands. Daily life on Aunt Em's farm, though imbued with warm relationships, is black and white; the fascinating land of Oz is in color. The scenery of the high plains is reduced to drab, two-dimensional sky, and all that matters is the foreground—the barn and chickens and farmhouse. As I grew up in Kansas, I absorbed the lessons of the movies and magazines, and I assumed that my native land around me was ordinary. I wanted to trade plain elm trees for the palm trees of television's *77 Sunset Strip* or *Adventures in Paradise*.

Sometimes when I was young, my unfashionable mid-western kingdom amazed me nonetheless. I loved looking at the first ridge of the Flint Hills west of town. The intense blue sky came down to a band of haze and then shaded, imperceptibly, into the purple hills themselves. (Later I learned the Flint Hills sit atop an ancient mountain range, the Nemahas.) The night sky of stars was a brilliant air-scape. When I was ten, I wanted to become an astronomer to fully grasp their existence. Some intangible experience surrounded me that was as completely real as long after-noons of sun. Perhaps it was simply beauty: The grand scale of sky—a manifestation of infinity itself—evoked ac-tive appreciation.

But it took many years for me to trust my own aesthetics and to see the full spectrum of colors in the Kansas sun-light.

First, I had children of my own. The media-free years of their early childhood was a recollection of my own enthusi-asms. A wasp nest *is* worth long scrutiny (and time stretched and curved to fit each day's discovery). Sand dredged from the river for a sandpile was a diary of the riv-er's travels. Tiny bits of quartz and flint and sandstone glit-tered on our fingers. We learned all the properties of dry, damp, and molded wet sand. Our back yard provided daily adventures with mud, bugs, wildflowers, cats, and blue jays. Following toddlers on their daily treks is an initiation into the mysteries of any place.

My second epiphany came when I accompanied the chil-dren to the local natural history museum. After the third and fourth trips I was not drawn to the La Brea tarpit ex-hibit with saber-toothed tigers and grinning wolves, or to the colorful tropical panorama of life zones. The exhibit I

Bridge over Wakarusa River, Margaret Whittemore

re-examined was in a far corner of the basement floor, findings from the Kansas River that flows through the Lawrence downtown, two miles from my house: a mastodon skull and tusks, a Folsom point, a giant ice age beaver skull, and an extinct bison skull with enormous horns. The mineralized brown bones came to life. The Folsom point fit itself onto the end of an oak shaft. Outside, the landscape shimmered beneath midday sun. Puddlings of terminal moraines and escarpments of limestone ocean bottoms would

never look the same. Encouraged by museum education
programs, I began to learn the bioregion that includes Kansas. The past opened under my feet, where underlying sedi-
ments preserve thousands of years of species. When mere
human measures of time are set aside, this land is as exotic
as Neptune.

The top layer in northeastern Kansas, glacial drift deposits, is the southernmost boundary of four continental
glaciers. The most extreme ice cover extended north of the
Kansas River and east to the Blue River. The valleys in this
area, now dotted with cornfields, once bulged with hundreds of feet of ice. In the north, the glacier was ten thousand feet thick, and it thinned as it reached its edge, Kansas, to two hundred feet. These spans require mental
acrobatics to envision. But evidence is there. The ice carried tons of rock and silt. Pink quartzlike boulders, relo-
cated from Minnesota outcroppings, are now common yard
ornaments. And these transients carry within them the
mystery of the Precambrian Age, the oldest geologic time,
when they were formed. The finer debris of retreating glaciers was loess, valuable topsoil that supports cattle and
grain. Our morning cereal comes from crushed Ice Age
rocks.

The habitat south of the ice sheet—most of Kansas—was
pine forest then, sustained by cool, damp weather patterns.
The climate was more temperate, and supported a variety
of large-scale mammals. These incredible *mega fauna* lived
in today's pastures and suburbs, in a different section of
time.

A cache of fossilized Ice Age bones washed into the Kansas River, perhaps during the 1951 flood, and spectacular
finds on sandbars are possible. A college student found a

mammoth skull, with curled tusks, buried in sand. My son Daniel found an extinct bison molar. Specimens of a forgotten bestiary abound underneath us, in a zoo fenced by stone.

There were herds of musk oxen and wild boars, mastodons, and huge bison two or three times the size of present day "buffalo." Giant sloths, as tall as houses, grazed on thorn trees. Terrible predators lived well: saber-toothed *smilodons* (several species), dire wolves, and most awesome, a cat-faced bear, *arctodus simus*. With only a minor adjustment in time (mammoth remains only 6,000 years old have been found in Kentucky) the place called Kansas becomes more interesting than anywhere on Earth today. The Ice Age continues to exist in the journals of paleontologists (like *The Mammoth Trumpet*), the collections of sandbar combers, and the minds of children growing up along the rivers. Maybe a tracing of those animals' spirits remains in the erratic, spinning particles that hover about these humid river valleys.

II. MOTHER'S DAY DRIVE

We head north, toward Lawrence,
into limestone country.
Highway slices stone,
exposing multitudes of skeletons,
hills filled with fossils—
crinoids, corals, clams.

Calcite
like these thick bones of mine
first formed grain by grain

from my mother's bloodstream.

Seedling cottonwoods
push up through rock cracks.
Layers of old ocean debris
hold up this spring's grass.

Glacial drift, bluffs of loess, and sand dunes of south-central Kansas are only recent surface decorations. The real foundation of the heartland is solid masses remaining from ancient swamps and oceans. Seawater covered almost all of the central continent hundreds of millions of years ago, and during long cycles, the seas rose and fell many times. Organic life began in the seas, and even now its remains sustain us.

In Kansas the sequence of geologic ages begins in the oldest eastern rocks and continues west. Southeastern Kansas surface rocks are solidified masses of coal swamps, 330 million years old. West of them are the Osage Cuestas, strata formed by Pennsylvanian seas, filled with clams and other marine life. Next, the Flint Hills are a band left from the Permian ocean (250 million years old). Bedrock for the rest of the state is a Cretacean system—chalk—that preserves more developed marine reptiles and fish. A spewing of eroded soil from the Rocky Mountains lies thickly over western Kansas, forming the expanses of level horizon, but underneath is this last sea of 63 million years ago.

A car trip across the state is 400 miles, but it also traces almost 300 million years from the Missouri border to Colorado. As elevation increases, rainfall declines; the damp gulf stream full of rainclouds has hastened the erosion of eastern Kansas, exposing older rock deposits, and this deepening valley uncovers even some Cambrian rocks further east into Missouri.

Fossil remains suggest dramas of survival and failure. A writer has daily reminders of survival and mortality in stones used for buildings, fences, and landscaping. The campus of Kansas State University is built of this "vernacular" limestone of eastern Kansas, and a nineteenth-century coffee shop where I like to write has rock walls filled with enigmatic fossil shells.

Pennsylvanian limestone includes corals, one-celled animals the size of wheat kernels (foraminifers), and many mollusks. These mussel-like animals appear to have dug into solid stone as a last hiding place. More unusual are the crinoids—sea animals that look like ferns. The segmented stems support a lily-like flower formed by tentacles. We can only wonder at the original coloring. Primitive sharks were marauders in the warm seas of this time, and a few last trilobites can be found here. These tiny crab ancestors flourished since early Cambrian times and died out gradually.

Also remarkable are fossils of the next period, the Cretaceous. Niobrara chalk in western Kansas holds in suspension many reptiles, large fish, and early birds. Swimming just below an apparently bland surface of wheatfields are mosasaurs, sea reptiles that resemble large snakes with fins. Another menace was the pleisiosaur, an alligator-like reptile. Many varieties of sharks developed to feed on clams, ammonites (related to today's nautilus), and sharp-toothed fishes. Humans would have no chance in this violent competition.

These forgotten animals, embedded in rock, provide mental sustenance for Kansans: they force the mind to reenvision the daily landscape; they testify to a dimension of time that carries each locale through remarkable trans- formations; they give perspective to individual life as well as the life cycle of an entire species. And the bones and shells of past ocean life soften, year by year, into topsoil that magically nourishes the present generation.

III. WEST

Here the sky gives clarity to each tree—
a gray hand on the horizon,
perpendicular on horizontal.

The long slope of miles
approaching the mountains,
moving always into blue blue haze.

Each tree a slow traveler on this road.

Returning to the ground level and present time, a singular beauty unfolds on the prairies. The buttes and parallel rhythm of ridges do not have the drama of cities or mountains or ocean, but nothing interrupts the sweep of sky around the horizon or diminishes its activities. The confrontation between earth and sky is as intense as the coastlines where water meets earth. And the unbroken sky is a transparent, barely physical element that teases the senses as well as the imagination. Untouchable sunsets create concentrations of colors: the air itself is tinged plum or cerise or brass.

The earth's constant rotation creates prevailing winds that sculpt snow drifts into crusty ocean waves. In June the

Torn by the Winds, Charles Rogers

wind shakes spores from pine trees and fills air with cotton from female cottonwood trees. Dust storms, volcanic ash, dried leaves, and hawks are all visible travelers on unseen currents. Wind, focused in tornado funnels or disseminated by Caribbean Gulf breezes, constantly exerts its invisible pressure. Every creature on the plains learns the effects of winds that, like God, no one has ever seen.

Fog, mist, drizzle, rain, hail, and cloudbursts have immediate tactile dimension, but the silent extremes of temperature do not. Snow blown by the northern winds is visible, but not the wind itself, nor the nightly tides of winter cold. Temperatures can reach forty degrees below zero (Lebanon, 1905). The searing heat of summer, up to 120 degrees, can create a womb-like warmth. During a hot spell the temperature hardly dips below ninety degrees, so the air presses against skin like a mother. Greetings among people, the prosaic comments on weather, are attempts to give verbal texture to unseen elements working freely on the land. Those who do not read the sky attentively pay a price. The blizzards, windstorms, burning heat, and even lightning cause fatalities each season.

In a prairie town there is no seaward or mountainside direction. But with the land exposed on all sides, the sky's four directions reveal distinct characteristics. The seasonal calendar is associated with north for winter, south for mild summer weather, and west for the next day's weather. Space and time join together; the immediate future can be seen in clouds forming on the western edge of the sky. Occasionally, time runs amok, and a storm blows yesterday's clouds back from the east. And of course the rising eastern sun, its rays uninterrupted, renews existence each day. No wonder Indian tribes base their understanding of creation on the four sacred directions and the place each being has within the hoop of the horizon. This circle is most whole on the grasslands.

IV. FRONTIER

Limestone blocks line the road
like walls of Assyrian fortresses.

We enter gates
to an old land
or hewn doors of hell—
the Great Desert.

Stacks of naked stones
mortared in place
guide us:
    black shale for old shallows, marshes,
    yellow limestone for sea bottoms.

Further below
peaks of Nemaha Mountains
lie buried in rain, wind, grit.
We pass carefully over the dead giant,
stepping on a grave.

At the center of the continent,
this so-called New World,
lie forest-heaved rocks, sediment,
these ruins.

The writer's conjuring of words comes naturally in this environment. So much is already dependent on the imagination, whether the distant Emerald City of Oz or prehistoric elephants or windstorms: fiction and natural history both must be construed. The Wicked Witch of the West on the movie screen is as plausible as the tornado that forces straw through a telephone pole. Though essentially unseen, the mind's effects have intense reality. The result of thought, language, is less tangible than rain, but also powerful. Invisible words, breathed from our mouths with soft bursts of air (bits of the sky element), join us to larger forces—our fel-

Willow Trees and Wheat, William Dickerson

low sky watchers, histories that occurred before us, and our own mysterious potential.

After discarding the flat images that recycle through Hollywood, the plains dweller revels in an unencumbered vista. The Great American Desert myth still keeps outsiders away. Few Americans really know this area, and none of them influence the media substantially. Few novels are set here and relatively few movies, plays, poems or television series.

Total originality is a necessity, anyway, for each person who tries to define the experience of sky-space. It has to be conceived within and comprehended by all parts of the brain. No one can communicate adequately the day's sunrise for another person, or describe polar air blowing through coat fabric. The expanses evoke active response, even participation. We breathe in portions of the sky, and conscious awareness of this breath unites the inner world of the mind to nature. Each individual must grapple with the concept of infinity on a daily basis.

The tallgrass prairie stirs the imagination not because it is empty, but because it is vast. It challenges any Ptolemaic misconception that humans are the center of the universe. A rancher mending fences in the Flint Hills is a dot against the sky, like the man depicted in a Chinese landscape painting is a diminutive part within the whole panorama of mountains and streams. The unspeakable scale of distance—as far as the eye can see and then farther still—challenges the utmost abilities of the mind. Kansas is a zone beyond the peopled horizon and beyond all time where only the best part of the human spirit walks, touching both earth and sky at once.

ACKNOWLEDGMENTS

Carl L. Becker: "Kansas," from *Essays in American History Dedicated to Frederick Jackson Turner* (New York: Henry Holt & Co., 1910), pp. 85–111.

William Allen White: "Kansas: A Puritan Survival," *Nation*, April 19, 1922, pp. 460–462.

W. G. Clugston: "Kansas, the Essence of Typical America," *Current History*, No. 25, October 1926, pp. 14–20.

May Williams Ward: "Sky-Mountain," *Contemporary Kansas Poetry*, ed. Helen Rhoda Hoopes (Lawrence, Kans.: Franklin Watts—The Book Nook, 1927), p. 120.

Karl A. Menninger: "Bleeding Kansans," *Kansas Magazine*, 1939, pp. 3–6.

Zula Bennington Greene: "The Cottonwood" and "The Prairie," from the *Topeka Capital*, reprinted in *Kansas Magazine*, 1945, back cover.

Kenneth Wiggins Porter: "Address to Kansans," *No Rain from These Clouds* (New York: John Day Company, 1946), pp. 123–124.

Milton S. Eisenhower: "The Strength of Kansas," *Kansas Magazine*, 1949, pp. 9–15.

Allan Nevins: *Kansas and the Stream of American Destiny* (Lawrence: University Press of Kansas, 1954).

William Stafford: "One Home," in *Stories That Could Be True* (New York: Harper & Row, 1977), p. 29. © 1977 by

236

ACKNOWL-
EDGMENTS

William Stafford. Reprinted with permission of Harper & Row, Publishers, Inc.

William Inge: "A Level Land," introduction to *The Plains States: Iowa, Kansas, Minnesota, Missouri, Nebraska, North Dakota, South Dakota*, by Evan Jones and the editors of Time-Life Books (New York: Time-Life Books, 1968), pp. 6–7.

Kenneth S. Davis: from "Portrait of a Changing Kansas," *Kansas Historical Quarterly*, Spring 1976, pp. 26–35.

Artful Goodtimes: "Breathing Kansas," *Tellus*, No. 5, 1979, pp. 2–4; and *Embracing the Earth* (Berkeley, Calif.: Homeward Press, 1984). © Artful Goodtimes.

Peg Wherry: "Straight Roads," *North American Review*, Vol. 267, No. 2, June 1982, pp. 4–7.

William Least Heat-Moon: "The Great Kansas Passage," Introduction to *The Four Seasons of Kansas* (Lawrence: University Press of Kansas, 1988), pp. 7–13.

Robert Day: "Not in Kansas Anymore," *Washington Post Magazine*, October 22, 1989, pp. 24–29. © Robert Day.

Denise Low: "Touching the Sky," original essay.

Illustrations are used with the permission of the Print Collection of the Spencer Museum of Art, University of Kansas.

INDEX

Farmers' Alliance, 127, 128, 133
First Capitol of Kansas,
    Whittemore (illus.), 130
"Flat," 153, 158, 159, 163, 165,
    180, 197, 200, 202, 221, 233
Flint Hills, 4
Flood, 153, 164, 165, 225
Fort Hays State University, 207
Free Silver furor, 70
Freesoilers, 134
Frontier, 12, 21, 22, 23, 24, 25, 26,
    29, 31, 37, 38, 42, 45, 68, 91,
    105, 109, 116, 131, 132, 133,
    135, 147, 173, 196
Fry, Provost-Marshal, 131
Funston, Fred, 141

Garden City, 183, 191
Garden of Sand (Thompson), 8
Garmon, John, 188
Ginsberg, Allen, 175
Girard, 80
Glass, Hugh, 142
Good Earth, The, Curry (illus.), 44
Goodtimes, Artful, 13, 175
Gould, Jay, 133
Grasshoppers, 4, 20, 26, 27, 30,
    47, 78, 131, 132, 171
Great American Desert, 168
"Great Common People," 10, 15,
    67, 69, 70, 78, 80, 81
"Great Kansas Passage," 175, 193,
    194
Greene, Zula Bennington, 97

Hagstrom, Jerry, 13
Haldeman-Julius, Emanuel, 9, 65,
    80
Haldeman-Julius, Marcet, 9
Hall, Arthur W., 235
Hardy, Thomas, 142

Harger, Charles, 7, 8
Harp, 83
Hay Meadow, Hall (illus.), 158
Hays, 78, 109, 196, 207
Hayseeds, Moralizers, & Methodists:
    The Twentieth Century Image of
    Kansas (Bader), 13
Haywood, C. Robert, 3
Hecht, Ben, 79
Hertzler, Arthur, 4
Holliday, Cyrus, 91
Howe, Edgar Watson, 9, 67, 79,
    93, 110, 142
Hughes, Langston, 124
Hugoton, 192
Huntoon, Mary, 235

Idealism, 22, 23, 24, 31, 32, 33, 34,
    38, 39, 40, 48, 49, 50, 57, 67,
    69, 73, 82, 87, 94, 124, 129,
    149
Illinois, 22, 69, 123
In Cold Blood (Capote), 203
"In God we trusted, in Kansas we
    busted," 26
Indiana, 22, 138
Individualism, 19, 23, 24, 25, 26,
    28, 29, 30, 41, 43, 45, 46, 49,
    109, 120, 123, 124, 125, 133,
    141, 146, 161
Industrial Wichita #2, Dickerson
    (illus.), 60
Ingalls, John J., 17, 46, 52, 93, 110,
    114, 132, 134, 138, 139, 147,
    162
Inge, Dean, 144
Inge, William, 124, 153
In the Kansas Senate, from the
    Balcony, Huntoon (illus.), 72
Iowa, 19, 22, 36, 47, 69, 79, 148,
    154, 179, 182, 185